VISUAL QUICKSTART GUIDE

W9-ARV-755

WordPress

Third Edition

JESSICA NEUMAN BECK • MATT BECK

 Peachpit Press

WordPress: Visual QuickStart Guide, Third Edition
Jessica Neuman Beck and Matt Beck

Peachpit Press
www.peachpit.com

To report errors, please send a note to errata@peachpit.com
Peachpit Press is a division of Pearson Education.

Project Editor: Valerie Witte
Production Editor: Tracey Croom
Copy Editor: Linda LaFlamme
Proofreader: Patricia J. Pane
Compositor: Aptara®, Inc.
Indexer: Rebecca Plunkett
Interior Design: Peachpit Press
Cover Design: RHDG / Riezebos Holzbaur Design Group, Peachpit Press
Logo Design: MINE™ www.minesf.com

Notice of Rights

Notice of Liability

Trademarks

ISBN-13: 978-0-321-95761-0
ISBN-10:   0-321-95761-X

9 8 7 6 5 4 3 2 1

Printed and bound in the United States of America

Special Thanks to:

Jessica and Matt would like to thank the editorial staff at Peachpit and the Portland WordPress community, without whom this book would not have been possible.

Thanks, guys!

Table of Contents

Introduction

WordPress is an open source blogging platform and content management system with the largest user base of any self-hosted blogging tool in the world. Users can set up a blog on WordPress.com or install WordPress with a hosting company or on a personal server, allowing for flexibility and easy customization. It's highly extensible, with a veritable treasure trove of add-ons and plug-ins available both in the official WordPress repository and elsewhere on the Internet. Because the project is open source, it's easy for developers to work with—and it's free!

In this introduction, we talk about what a blog is and how to use it. We'll tell you a little more about WordPress and give you an overview of new WordPress features. We'll also explore the differences between WordPress.org and WordPress.com to help you decide which one is right for you.

In this book, we'll be focusing on the self-hosted version of WordPress available at WordPress.org. This version offers the most flexibility and customization options. However, many of the usage tutorials are applicable to both self-hosted WordPress installations and WordPress.com blogs, so if you're new to WordPress, read on!

Blogs Explained

A *blog* is a Web site that displays posts or articles in a sequential order, with the newest posts appearing first. The word "blog" comes from *Weblog*, itself a contraction of *Web* and *log*.

Blogs began as online journals, usually featuring a single author writing about a specific topic or interest. Blogs have expanded, however, and now encompass news sites, magazine-style sites, and even corporate Web sites, in addition to personal journals.

Blogs often fill a niche, focusing on a particular subject, and often encourage participation by enabling comments on articles or posts.

Many sites are built on blogging platforms like WordPress because the interface for adding posts and pages is easy for nontechnical users to master.

The blog format tends toward the following:

- A new page is automatically generated for each post.

- Each post is defined by one or more categories.

- Posts can be further categorized by tags.
- Posts can be read sequentially or browsed in archives by date, category, or tag.

Design and layout are dictated by a predefined template or theme; changes to the theme affect the look and feel of the site but do not affect content (making it easy to modify a site's look).

Anatomy of a WordPress Blog

While blogs can vary widely in layout, most contain these six basic segments. We're using the default WordPress theme as an example of a typical blog layout **Ⓐ**. The basic segments are:

- **Header**: This section usually includes the blog's name and a graphic such as a logo.

- **Tagline (optional)**: The tagline or slogan often gives the reader a better idea of what the blog is about. The WordPress default tagline is "Just another WordPress weblog."

- **Navigation**: This consists of internal links to the different sections of the site, such as Archives, About, and Home.

- **Content**: This section changes depending on what section of the blog is being viewed; for example, on the home page the content may be an overview of the latest posts, while the contact page would include information and perhaps a form for getting in touch with the blog's author.

- **Sidebar**: Additional navigation may be located here, as well as snippets of code known as *widgets*, which may contain information such as the author's latest Twitter posts, polls, an overview of recent comments, or photos recently posted to Flickr.

- **Footer**: This section usually contains copyright and design information.

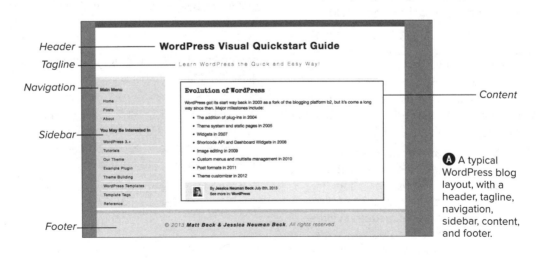

Ⓐ A typical WordPress blog layout, with a header, tagline, navigation, sidebar, content, and footer.

In addition, each post's page contains information specific to the post, such as the time and date of posting, the author, the categories and/or tags, and (if comments are enabled) a place for readers to contribute their thoughts.

What's New in This Edition

WordPress regularly releases updates to its core platform, debuting new features, security fixes, and stability increases in controlled bursts. After WordPress 2.1, the development team began releasing updates on a regular schedule, roughly every three to four months. Major updates are named after famous Jazz artists.

WordPress 3.0 (named after Thelonious Monk) saw a major overhaul of the WordPress platform, merging WordPress MU (Multi User) with the WordPress core and making it possible to manage multiple installations of WordPress from one main installation. It also included many new features, such as:

- Custom menus
- Custom headers
- Custom backgrounds
- Contextual help
- Support for custom post types and custom taxonomies

Since the 3.0 update, WordPress has continued to evolve, and has added more new features:

- Internal linking
- The admin bar
- Post formats
- A full-screen editor
- A refreshed administrative UI
- Improved revisions
- New audio/visual APIs

In addition, the WordPress team has decided to release a new default theme every year. These themes will take advantage of the latest WordPress features and have been named after the year in which they were released (Twenty Ten, Twenty Eleven, and the latest, Twenty Thirteen). These default themes are included in core updates and are available to both self-hosted WordPress users and users on WordPress.com.

WordPress.org Versus WordPress.com

There are two distinctly different versions of WordPress: the downloadable, open source version found at WordPress.org  and the hosted version at WordPress.com **B**.

The self-installed version of WordPress, WordPress.org, is the most common. You install it on your own Web server (most likely on a hosting account), and you have full access to both the source code and the database where your information is stored.

WordPress.com is a free, hosted blog service (meaning you can use it without a hosting account). Setup, upgrades, spam protection, and backups are all taken care of by the WordPress.com service, but you do not get FTP or shell access and cannot modify your site's PHP. WordPress.com also has some content restrictions (for example, paid or sponsored post content is not allowed).

A WordPress.org is the open-source, self-hosted variety of WordPress.

B WordPress.com is a free, hosted blog service.

Here's a handy reference table so you can quickly see the difference between WordPress.org and WordPress.com.

At first glance, a blog hosted on WordPress.com is similar to the self-hosted version. Like other hosted blogging services, such as TypePad and Blogger, WordPress.com allows basic theme customization (from a preapproved set of themes) and lets users add pages, sidebars, and widgets. The free account takes only seconds to set up. Free users are given a subdomain at [yourname]. wordpress.com and currently get 3 GB of storage for images and media. Such options as theme styling, suppression of WordPress text ads, and a custom domain name are available for a fee. It's a good solution for beginners looking to have an online presence without owning a domain name or paying for Web hosting.

If you're an advanced user, a Web professional, or someone using WordPress for a business, however, you need to be able to modify and customize your site to create a unique brand experience. That's where the self-hosted version of WordPress from WordPress.org comes in. With it, you have full control over every aspect of your site. You'll be able to build your own theme, install plug-ins, and easily modify your design. This is particularly important if you want to use WordPress as a lightweight content management system (commonly referred to as a CMS) rather than "just a blog."

With a self-hosted WordPress installation, you can create a full-featured site that functions in whatever way you want it to, limited only by your imagination (and your knowledge of theme building).

TIP **If you're still not sure which version of WordPress is right for you, sign up for a free account at WordPress.com to give the hosted service a test drive. Even if you don't end up using your WordPress.com blog, a WordPress.com account can be used to tie in with some fun plug-ins for the self-hosted version of WordPress, like Jetpack. We talk more about installing the Jetpack plug-in in Chapter 15, "More Ways to Customize WordPress."**

Table I.1 Comparison of WordPress.org and WordPress.com

WordPress.org	WordPress.com
Free to use	Free to use basic version
Installed on your own Web server or Web-hosting account	Hosted on WordPress.com
Ads are not included by default (although you may choose to run your own ads)	Ads may be displayed on your blog
	Limited selection of plug-ins and themes
Thousands of plug-ins and themes	Features may be extended by paying for premium services
Fully customizable	Number of users is limited
Unlimited user accounts	Content restrictions apply
No content restrictions	Requires no setup aside from choosing theme and entering content
Requires setup and maintenance	
Analytic statistics offered by plug-ins	Built-in analytic statistics

First Steps

This chapter will walk you through the process of getting started with WordPress. From installation to setup, we'll give you the knowledge you need to get up and running with a new WordPress-powered site.

We'll detail the minimum requirements you'll need from your Web host in order to ensure compatibility with WordPress. Then we'll give you step-by-step instructions for setting up WordPress using Fantastico and other installers; creating a MySQL database both in a hosting control panel and in phpMyAdmin; and using the WordPress installer.

You're just steps away from your first WordPress-powered Web site!

Setting Up WordPress

There are several ways to set up WordPress, and the one you choose will depend on the type of Web host you use. Most hosting companies offer WordPress installers or installation assistance—some are even preconfigured to use WordPress right out of the box! If you're installing WordPress on an existing hosting plan, it's worthwhile to find out what WordPress installation options they offer.

If your hosting account uses the very popular cPanel control panel, odds are you have access to the Fantastico De Luxe autoinstaller, which allows you to easily install a number of different applications—including WordPress. For more information on Fantastico, go to www.netenberg.com/fantastico.php.

If you don't have Fantastico, don't worry: We will walk you through a manual setup process in which you first create the database that WordPress will use to store all your blog posts and pages, and then run the WordPress installer to set up the WordPress platform.

Minimum Requirements for Running WordPress

Most modern hosting providers and personal Unix/Linux hosting setups can handle running WordPress.

WordPress will run on Windows servers and Internet Information Services (IIS), but Linux and Apache are recommended for the Apache mod_rewrite module's ability to create easy-to-read friendly URLs (see the section "Permalinks" in Chapter 3, "Settings").

The Apache mod_rewrite module is required for WordPress Multi-Site. For more information on Multi-Site, see Chapter 14, "One Installation, Multiple Blogs."

The recommended server setup:

- PHP version 5.2.4 or greater
- MySQL version 5.0 or greater

For a comprehensive rundown of server requirements, visit http://wordpress.org/about/requirements/.

A Hosting Account or Your Own Server?

Unless you anticipate high traffic or need full control of your server for reasons unrelated to WordPress, setting up your own Web server probably isn't worth the trouble. Most hosting companies support WordPress, and hosting is generally cheaper to buy than it is to maintain.

We recommend finding a reliable, affordable Web host that has lots of happy customers. If you're choosing a new hosting company, check to see if they offer WordPress automatic install and upgrades. This will save you lots of time in the future and ensure that you're always running the latest version of WordPress.

WordPress maintains a list of hosting providers they recommend at http://wordpress.org/hosting/.

If you already have your own Web server, you can easily configure it to run WordPress. Make sure you adhere to the minimum requirements and follow the instructions in this chapter for a new WordPress installation.

Using an Installer

If your hosting company has an autoinstaller for WordPress, setup is a breeze! The autoinstaller takes care of creating the required database where WordPress will store all of your settings, posts, and pages, and it creates all the files and directories that WordPress needs to run as well as setting basic configuration options.

If you aren't sure what your hosting company offers in the way of autoinstallers, ask them.

To install WordPress using Fantastico:

1. In your browser, navigate to the URL of your cPanel (control panel) and log in using your administrative user account and password 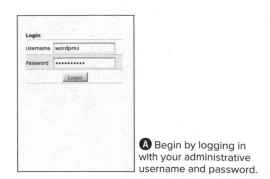.

2. Once you are logged in, locate and select the smiley face icon labeled Fantastico De Luxe.

   The arrangement of your cPanel windows varies from hosting company to hosting company, but this icon is most likely to be located under Software/Services 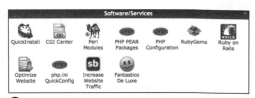.

3. In the left panel under Blogs, click WordPress to start the installation process .

A Begin by logging in with your administrative username and password.

B The cPanel menu lets you control many aspects of your hosting account.

C The Fantastico autoinstaller is an easy way to set up WordPress.

WordPress

Short description: WordPress is a blogging software with a focus on ease of use, elegance, performance, and standards with a huge selection of themes and plugins.
Homepage: http://wordpress.org/

WordPress support forum
(We are not associated with the support forum)

New Installation (3.5)
Disk space required: 14.86 MB
Disk space available: 1486.5 MB

Current installations:

None

D Click the New Installation link.

WordPress

Install WordPress (1/3)

Installation location

Install on domain demo.wpvisualquickstart.com

Install in directory

Leave empty to install in the root directory of the domain (access example: http://domain/).
Enter only the directory name to install in a directory (for **http://domain/name/** enter **name** only). This directory SHOULD NOT exist, it will be automatically created!

Admin access data

Administrator username (you need this to enter the protected admin area)   myname

Password (you need this to enter the protected admin area)   mypassword

Base configuration

Admin nickname   Admin

Admin e-mail (your email address)   author@wpvisualquickstart.co

Site name   demo.wpvisualquickstart.com

Description   WordPress Visual Quickstart

Install WordPress

E Fantastico WordPress installer 1/3 (screen 1 of 3).

4. The first WordPress installer screen shows requirements and previously installed copies of WordPress for your hosting account (if any). To create a new WordPress installation, click the New Installation link **D**.

5. Fill out the fields under Install WordPress (1/3), paying careful attention to the onscreen instructions **E**.

Here's where you will set a username and password for your WordPress admin account and provide general details about your site. The site name and description you enter here will be displayed on your Web site and can be changed later—but your administrative username and password can't, so choose carefully! After completing all the fields, click the Install WordPress button to continue.

6. The next screen gives you information about the installation that Fantastico is going to create for you. Look this information over carefully. If everything looks correct, click Finish Installation **F**.

continues on next page

Install WordPress (2/3)
The MySQL database and MySQL user **wordpres_wrdp2** will be created and used for this installation.

- You chose to install in the main directory of the domain **demo.wpvisualquickstart.com**.
- The access URL will be: **http://demo.wpvisualquickstart.com/**.

Click on **Finish installation** to continue.

Finish installation

F Fantastico WordPress installer 2/3 (screen 2 of 3).

That's it! WordPress is now installed. The final installer screen recaps the settings you selected during the setup process and provides a URL to your new WordPress installation **G**.

TIP If you aren't sure whether your hosting account uses cPanel or Fantastico, this information is usually included in the welcome email you received from the hosting company when you signed up for your account.

TIP Fantastico can be used to install many more applications besides WordPress. Your available options will vary depending on your hosting company, but common options include shopping cart software, other blogging platforms, forums, and more.

Install WordPress (3/3)

/home/wordpres/public_html/demo/wp-config.php configured
/home/wordpres/public_html/demo/data.sql configured

Please notice:

We only offer auto-installation and auto-configuration of **WordPress** but do not offer any kind of support.

You need a username and a password to enter the admin area. Your username is **myname**. Your password is **mypassword** The full URL to the admin area (**Bookmark this!**): http://demo.wpvisualquickstart.com/wp-admin/

DO NOT REMOVE the file named fantastico_fileslist.txt from the installation directory. It is used for uninstalling this application.

Back to WordPress overview

Email the details of this installation to:

Send E-mail

G Fantastico WordPress installer 3/3 (screen 3 of 3).

Setting Up WordPress Using Other Installers

Our example uses the Fantastico De Luxe installer via cPanel, a common hosting control panel. However, many other hosting companies use other control panels and installers. Some hosts have even built their own installers, which can further simplify the process.

If your hosting company doesn't use cPanel on its servers, contact your hosting company's support staff or search through their online support pages to find out how they support WordPress installation.

MySQL® Database Wizard

[Video Tutorial]

A Under Database, click MySQL Database Wizard to open it.

Step 1: Create A Database

New Database: wordpress ✓

[Next Step]

B Step 1 of the MySQL Database Wizard is creating a database.

Step 2: Create Database Users:

Username: wpuser ✓ *Seven characters max

Password:

Password Strength:
Very Weak (0/100)   [Generate Password]

Password (Again):

[Next Step]

C Step 2 of the MySQL Database Wizard is creating database users.

MySQL® Database Wizard

Added the database wordpres_wordpress.

Step 2: Create Database U

Username: wpu

Password Generator

gN2x,6HSzHW]
Password Strength:
Very Strong (100/100)

[Regenerate]

Uppercase: ☑
Lowercase: ☑
Numbers: ☑
Symbols: ☑

Password Length: 12

Password (Again):

[Use Password] [Cancel]

[Next Step]

D The MySQL Database Wizard generates a password for you

Setting Up a Database

WordPress requires a MySQL database to store the information for your site, such as your blog posts, page content, usernames and passwords, custom post type information, and more.

If you use an installer like Fantastico to set up WordPress, it will create this database for you automatically. If not, these instructions will help you set one up yourself.

To set up a MySQL database using a hosting control panel:

1. In your browser, navigate to the URL of your cPanel (control panel) and log in using your administrative username and password.

2. In the Databases section, select MySQL Database Wizard **A**.

3. In the first screen of the Database Wizard, enter the name of the database you would like to create. In our example we are calling the database *wordpress,* but you can use any unique name you want. Click Next Step to continue **B**.

4. In Step 2 of the Database Wizard, you will need to create a MySQL username and password that will allow WordPress to store and retrieve all the information it needs to function. Enter a username (*wpuser* in our example), and click Generate Password **C**.

5. In the pop-up window that appears, you will see that cPanel has automatically created a password for you. We recommend using this automatically generated password for security purposes, because it's difficult to guess **D**. Click Use Password to populate the password fields on this screen, and click Next Step to continue to the next screen.

continues on next page

You can create a password manually, but the random password is usually a better choice. You will not need to type this password to log in to WordPress or anything else; it's only needed during database setup, so don't worry about it being hard to remember.

6. At the top of the screen you will now see the actual username and password that were created **E**. Note that in our example the *wordpres_* prefix has been added to the wpuser username we typed in previously. Make a note of the username and password for use when you install WordPress later.

   This screen also asks you what permissions you want to give the MySQL user for the database you are creating. Click All Privileges to check all the boxes, and then click Next Step to continue.

   A confirmation screen will appear telling you that the user has been added to the database **F**. Your MySQL database has been created and a user account has been added to it for WordPress to utilize. You can now move on to "Installing WordPress."

TIP In step 4, you saw "Added database *name-of-database*" at the top of the screen; note that in our example, the database that was created is actually called *wordpres_wordpress*, not *wordpress* as we typed it back in **B**. This is because cPanel hosting accounts are almost always used in a shared server setup, which means that many other people have accounts on the same Web server. The *wordpres_* prefix keeps our database information separate from other users on the system. Make note of the actual database name for use when you install WordPress later.

E Step 3 of the MySQL Database Wizard is adding the user to the database.

F Step 4 of the MySQL Database Wizard is completing the task.

❖ Create new database: ⑦
❌No Privileges

G If you see No Privileges, you won't be able to use this method of setting up the MySQL database.

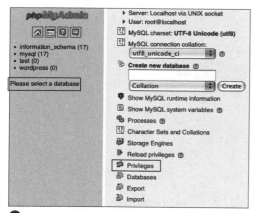

H You'll use this menu to create your database.

Click here to *set up MySQL Database*

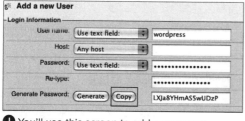

I Click Add A New User.

Add a new User
Login Information
User name:	Use text field:	wordpress
Host:	Any host	
Password:	Use text field:	●●●●●●●●●●●●●●
Re-type:		●●●●●●●●●●●●●●
Generate Password:	Generate Copy	LXJa8YHmASSwUDzP

J You'll use this screen to add a new user.

ⓘ **You have added a new user.**

K You'll see this confirmation screen after you add a new user.

To set up a MySQL Database using phpMyAdmin:

1. Sign in to phpMyAdmin on your hosting account. The URL you'll need to use for this task varies from host to host.

2. Look for the Create New Database section. If you see a red X and the words *No Privileges*, you won't be able to use this method of setting up the MySQL database **G**.

   This is fairly common on shared server hosting, such as cPanel. Don't worry; you can still use phpMyAdmin to administer databases, but you'll have to create the database using the tools provided by your hosting company.

   However, if you see a blank text box below Create New Database, click Privileges to set up your database **H**.

3. Once you've displayed the Privileges section of the database administration screen, click Add A New User to continue **I**.

4. Enter a username (*wordpress* in our example), and click Generate. Next, click Copy to let the system generate a strong password for you automatically **J**. You could manually enter a password here, but we don't recommend it.

5. Make a note of the username and password so you'll have them when you install WordPress. Confirm that Create Database With Same Name And Grant All Privileges is selected under Database For User, and click Go.

   You should see a confirmation screen telling you that you have added a new user **K**. If you do, that means the database was created correctly and you can now move on to the next section.

Installing WordPress

WordPress boasts the "famous 5-minute installation process," which means you'll be up and running in no time. Follow these easy steps to install WordPress on your server.

To run the WordPress installer:

1. In your browser, go to www.wordpress. org/download/ and click the Download WordPress button **A**.

2. Download and extract the ZIP file containing the WordPress installation files.

3. Open your favorite FTP client and enter the settings provided to you by your hosting company to access your server.

4. You should see a list of files and directories on your local computer as well as on your Web server **B**. Navigate to the directory on your server where you want to install WordPress.

5. Find the extracted files from the ZIP file you downloaded in step 2; select them and drag them into the directory on your server where you want to install WordPress to upload the files **C**. Depending on the speed of your Internet connection, this process may take several minutes to complete.

continues on page 12

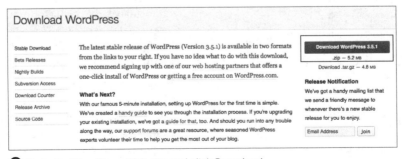

A Go to the WordPress Web site and click Download.

Name ▲	Size	Date
.DS_Store	8 KB	Friday, June 7, 2013 1:09 AM
▶ wordpress	--	Jan 24, 2013 7:53 PM
wordpress-3.5.1.zip	5.4 MB	Jun 7, 2013 12:34 AM

Name ▲	Size	Date
▶ cgi-bin	--	6/7/13
index.php	395 B	1/8/12
license.txt	20 KB	5/6/12
readme.html	9 KB	6/7/13
wp-activate.php	5 KB	11/17/12
▶ wp-admin	--	12/11/12
wp-blog-header.php	271 B	1/8/12
wp-comments-post.php	4 KB	4/10/12
wp-config-sample.php	3 KB	11/1/10
wp-config.php	4 KB	6/7/13
▶ wp-content	--	6/7/13
wp-cron.php	3 KB	9/23/12
▶ wp-includes	--	12/11/12
wp-links-opml.php	2 KB	10/23/10
wp-load.php	2 KB	10/26/12
wp-login.php	29 KB	11/30/12
wp-mail.php	8 KB	9/24/12
wp-settings.php	10 KB	11/22/12
wp-signup.php	18 KB	9/11/12
wp-trackback.php	4 KB	1/8/12
xmlrpc.php	3 KB	9/11/12

B In your FTP client, navigate to the directory where you want to install WordPress.

Name ▲	Size	Date
index.php	4 KB	Jan 8, 2012 4:01 PM
license.txt	20 KB	May 6, 2012 7:28 AM
readme.html	12 KB	Jan 24, 2013 7:50 PM
wp-activate.php	8 KB	Nov 17, 2012 2:11 PM
▶ wp-admin	--	Jan 24, 2013 7:53 PM
wp-blog-header.php	4 KB	Jan 8, 2012 4:01 PM
wp-comments-post.php	4 KB	Apr 10, 2012 5:21 PM
wp-config-sample.php	4 KB	Nov 1, 2010 2:45 PM
▶ wp-content	--	Jan 24, 2013 7:53 PM
wp-cron.php	4 KB	Sep 23, 2012 4:57 PM
▶ wp-includes	--	Jan 24, 2013 7:53 PM
wp-links-opml.php	4 KB	Oct 23, 2010 12:17 PM
wp-load.php	4 KB	Oct 26, 2012 7:40 PM
wp-login.php	33 KB	Nov 30, 2012 12:41 PM
wp-mail.php	8 KB	Sep 25, 2012 5:26 AM
wp-settings.php	12 KB	Nov 22, 2012 8:52 AM
wp-signup.php	20 KB	Sep 11, 2012 12:27 PM
wp-trackback.php	4 KB	Jan 8, 2012 4:01 PM
xmlrpc.php	4 KB	Sep 11, 2012 8:11 PM

Name ▲	Size	Date
▶ cgi-bin	--	6/7/13

C Drag the extracted files to the installation directory.

6. When the upload is complete, take a quick look at the list of files on your server to make sure everything uploaded correctly **D**.

7. In your browser, navigate to the URL of your new site (this will be your main URL if you installed WordPress in the main directory, or a URL with a slash and a folder name if you installed it in a subdirectory). You should see the first screen of the WordPress installer **E**. Click Create A Configuration File to continue. If you get an error that says "Sorry, I can't write to the directory" at this stage, you'll need to proceed to step 8 to modify the file system permissions on the server. If you don't see an error message, skip to step 10.

Name ▲	Size	Date
index.php	4 KB	Jan 8, 2012 4:01 PM
license.txt	20 KB	May 6, 2012 7:28 AM
readme.html	12 KB	Jan 24, 2013 7:50 PM
wp-activate.php	8 KB	Nov 17, 2012 2:11 PM
▶ wp-admin	--	Jan 24, 2013 7:53 PM
wp-blog-header.php	4 KB	Jan 8, 2012 4:01 PM
wp-comments-post.php	4 KB	Apr 10, 2012 5:21 PM
wp-config-sample.php	4 KB	Nov 1, 2010 2:45 PM
▶ wp-content	--	Jan 24, 2013 7:53 PM
wp-cron.php	4 KB	Sep 23, 2012 4:57 PM
▶ wp-includes	--	Jan 24, 2013 7:53 PM
wp-links-opml.php	4 KB	Oct 23, 2010 12:17 PM
wp-load.php	4 KB	Oct 26, 2012 7:40 PM
wp-login.php	33 KB	Nov 30, 2012 12:41 PM
wp-mail.php	8 KB	Sep 25, 2012 5:26 AM
wp-settings.php	12 KB	Nov 22, 2012 8:52 AM
wp-signup.php	20 KB	Sep 11, 2012 12:27 PM
wp-trackback.php	4 KB	Jan 8, 2012 4:01 PM
xmlrpc.php	4 KB	Sep 11, 2012 8:11 PM

Name ▲	Size	Date
▶ cgi-bin	--	6/7/13
index.php	395 B	1/8/12
license.txt	20 KB	5/6/12
readme.html	9 KB	6/7/13
wp-activate.php	5 KB	11/17/12
▶ wp-admin	--	12/11/12
wp-blog-header.php	271 B	1/8/12
wp-comments-post.php	4 KB	4/10/12
wp-config-sample.php	3 KB	11/1/10
wp-config.php	4 KB	6/7/13
▶ wp-content	--	6/7/13
wp-cron.php	3 KB	9/23/12
▶ wp-includes	--	12/11/12
wp-links-opml.php	2 KB	10/23/10
wp-load.php	2 KB	10/26/12
wp-login.php	29 KB	11/30/12
wp-mail.php	8 KB	9/24/12
wp-settings.php	10 KB	11/22/12
wp-signup.php	18 KB	9/11/12
wp-trackback.php	4 KB	1/8/12
xmlrpc.php	3 KB	9/11/12

D Make sure the WordPress files and directories have been uploaded.

There doesn't seem to be a wp-config.php file. I need this before we can get started.

Need more help? We got it.

You can create a wp-config.php file through a web interface, but this doesn't work for all server setups. The safest way is to manually create the file.

[Create a Configuration File]

E Click the Create A Configuration File button.

8. Find the file wp-config-sample in the downloaded and extracted directory on your local computer and rename the file **wp-config.php**. Open the file in a text editor such as Notepad, BBEdit, or TextMate, and enter the database settings as described in the file under the comment `// ** MySQL settings - You can get this from your web host ** //` (you'll need the MySQL username and password as well as the database name). Once that's done, use your FTP client to upload the new file to your server.

9. Reload your new site in your browser to continue. (Steps 10 and 11 deal with an alternate method of creating the wp-config.php file, so you can skip them and go to step 12.)

10. If your server's permission settings will allow you to automatically create the wp-config.php file, you'll be looking at the Welcome to WordPress page. Click Let's Go! to continue **F**.

continues on next page

F Click the Let's Go! button to continue.

11. Enter all your database connection details: You'll need to know the name of the database as well as the MySQL username and password you created earlier **G**. The odds are high that the database host will stay set to localhost. If you intend to install only one blog, the default table prefix setting of wp_ is fine. If you intend to run multiple copies of WordPress out of the same database, you'll need to change the table prefix to something unique. When you finish, click Submit.

12. You should see a confirmation page telling you that the first part of the installation is complete. Click Run The Install to continue **H**.

Ⓦ **WORDPRESS**

Below you should enter your database connection details. If you're not sure about these, contact your host.

Database Name	wordpress	The name of the database you want to run WP in.
User Name	username	Your MySQL username
Password	password	...and your MySQL password.
Database Host	localhost	You should be able to get this info from your web host, if localhost does not work.
Table Prefix	wp_	If you want to run multiple WordPress installations in a single database, change this.

Submit

G Complete these fields and click Submit.

Ⓦ **WORDPRESS**

All right sparky! You've made it through this part of the installation. WordPress can now communicate with your database. If you are ready, time now to...

Run the install

H Click Run The Install.

(W) WORDPRESS

Welcome

Welcome to the famous five minute WordPress installation process! You may want to browse the ReadMe documentation at your leisure. Otherwise, just fill in the information below and you'll be on your way to using the most extendable and powerful personal publishing platform in the world.

Information needed

Please provide the following information. Don't worry, you can always change these settings later.

Site Title	WordPress Visual QuickStart
Username	myname
	Usernames can have only alphanumeric characters, spaces, underscores, hyphens, periods and the @ symbol.
Password, twice A password will be automatically generated for you if you leave this blank.	
	Strength indicator
	Hint: The password should be at least seven characters long. To make it stronger, use upper and lower case letters, numbers and symbols like ! " ? $ % ^ &).
Your E-mail	author@wpvisualquickstart.con
	Double-check your email address before continuing.
Privacy	☑ Allow search engines to index this site.

[Install WordPress]

❶ After you enter the required information, click Install WordPress.

13. Under Information needed, enter the title of your site, a username for your admin account, the password, and your email address ❶. If you do not enter a password here, WordPress will automatically generate a random password for you to use. (You can also select whether you wish your site to be indexed by search engines.) The title you enter here will almost always be displayed on your site, and you can change it later. Be sure that you've entered a valid email address for yourself, and click Install WordPress.

14. On the Success screen ❷, if you did not set your own password, take careful note of the automatically generated password for the admin account. You will need this password the first time you log in. Click Log In to continue.

continues on next page

(W) WORDPRESS

Success!

WordPress has been installed. Were you expecting more steps? Sorry to disappoint.

Username	myname
Password	jLTeVpdadugn *Note that password* carefully! It is a *random* password that was generated just for you.

[Log In]

❷ WordPress has installed successfully, so you can click Log In to continue.

15. On the login screen, enter **admin** for the username, and then enter the password (from step 14). Click Log In to access your WordPress site .

16. If you did not set your own password, you should see a highlighted message (at the top of the dashboard) letting you know that you're using the automatically generated password and giving you the option to change it. If you're satisfied with the password that was created for you, click No Thanks, Do Not Remind Me Again. If you want to change that password, click Yes, Take Me To My Profile Page .

K Enter your username and password, and then click Log In.

> **Notice:** You're using the auto-generated password for your account. Would you like to change it to something easier to remember?
>
> Yes, take me to my profile page | No thanks, do not remind me again

L To change the password, click Yes, Take Me To My Profile Page.

17. On the profile page, enter your new password twice ⓜ. WordPress will help by letting you know the strength of the new password as you type. When you're satisfied with your password, click Update Profile.

The page will refresh, and you should see a confirmation that the user information was updated. Your password has now been changed. WordPress is set up and ready to be configured.

TIP **In case you don't already have an FTP client on your computer, several free clients are available that work quite well. If you use the Firefox browser, you can use the popular FireFTP add-on. For Mac users, Cyberduck is a popular free choice, while LeechFTP is a popular free choice for Windows.**

To change your password, enter your new password twice.

New Password		*If you would like to change the password type a new one. Otherwise leave this blank.*
		Type your new password again.
	Strength indicator	*Hint: The password should be at least seven characters long. To make it stronger, use upper and lower case letters, numbers and*

symbols like ! " ? $ % ^ &).

Update Profile

ⓜ Changing the password.

Putting It All Together

1. **Install WordPress.** What method did you use to install WordPress? How do you know if your installation is working?

2. **Check your inbox.** Did you get an email from WordPress?

3. **Sign in to WordPress using the account you created during the installation**. Do you see your Dashboard?

4. **Take a look at your front-facing Web site by visiting your URL.** What do you see on the homepage?

Getting Familiar with WordPress

Now is a good time to settle down with WordPress and get comfortable with the way it works. In this chapter, we'll give you an overview of how a WordPress-powered site functions.

We'll walk you through logging in and navigating the Dashboard and the Admin Bar, which lets you administer your site from the front end while you are logged in; we'll teach you how to use the feature pointers and contextual help to find quick answers to any questions that may arise; and we'll show you how to delete the default content that is included with every new WordPress installation.

Upgrading from a previous version of WordPress? No problem! We'll talk about upgrading automatically and via FTP to be sure you're always running the latest, greatest version of WordPress.

How WordPress Works: An Overview

A WordPress site consists of two primary components: the WordPress back-end administration system and the front-end Web site that is displayed to people visiting your URL. The front end can be easily customized using themes, but the back-end administrative dashboard looks the same for most users (although you do have the ability to customize it, the dashboard is highly functional right out of the box).

When we talk about *using* WordPress, we're usually referring to the back-end system where content is created and managed.

To log in to WordPress:

1. The direct link to your dashboard is your_site.com/wp-admin. If you're already logged in, visiting that link will bring you directly to your Dashboard. Otherwise you will be prompted to log in.

2. Enter your username and password and click Log In to access your WordPress Dashboard **Ⓐ**. If you're not on a public or shared computer and would like to save your login information for next time, check the Remember Me check box.

TIP Not sure if you're logged in? Look for the Admin Bar at the top of your screen. If it's there, you're logged in and can use the quick links to access various sections of your site. For more about the Admin Bar, read on!

Ⓐ Type your username and password, and click Log In.

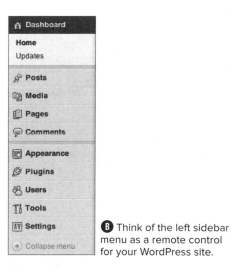

A The Dashboard gives you quick tools to accomplish common tasks and provides basic but useful information about your site.

Finding Your Way Around the Dashboard

The first page you see when you log in to WordPress is the Dashboard **A**. The Dashboard has several modules; the default set provides an easy way for you to see the current status of your site, create a quick post, and keep up to date on news and information generated by the developers of WordPress and the WordPress community. The sidebar menu in the Dashboard gives you quick access to all the sections, tools, and settings for your site **B**.

B Think of the left sidebar menu as a remote control for your WordPress site.

- Click the Dashboard button at the top of the left-side navigation at any time to view the main Dashboard overview screen. This will also expand the Dashboard sidebar submenu. If there are updates to the WordPress core or any of your plug-ins, you'll see them indicated here **C**.

- The Right Now dashboard widget **D** provides a quick overview of your site: the number of posts, pages, categories and tags, the number of comments, and your current theme and number of active widgets. If you're running the Akismet spam-catching plug-in, those stats will appear in the Right Now section as well.

- QuickPress provides a scaled-down, simple interface for creating a new blog post. It's especially handy for quickly saving drafts of posts to be added to the site later **E**.

- Recent Comments are shown in the Recent Comments section **F**. If pingbacks are enabled on your site, you will see these in this section as well (see "Discussion" in Chapter 3, "Settings").

🏠 **Dashboard**

Home

Updates **4**

C Clicking the Dashboard button will reveal a submenu that contains useful links and notifications of updates.

Right Now

Content		Discussion	
33	Posts	10	Comments
11	Pages	10	Approved
8	Categories	0	Pending
64	Tags	0	Spam

Theme **Our Theme** with **3 Widgets**

You are using **WordPress 3.6**

Akismet has protected your site from 96,991 spam comments already. There's nothing in your spam queue at the moment.

D The Right Now widget is a quick way to get some basic info about your site.

QuickPress

Enter title here

📷 Add Media

Tags (separate with commas)

Save Draft   Reset   Publish

E The QuickPress dashboard widget allows you to make simple blog entries but doesn't include such advanced options as categories, scheduling, or excerpts.

Recent Comments

From Mr WordPress on Hello world! #
Hi, this is a comment. To delete a comment, just log in and view the post's comments. There you will have ...

All | Pending (0) | Approved | Spam (0) | Trash (0)

F Your recent comments and pingbacks are listed in the Recent Comments widget.

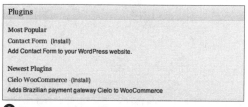

Recent Drafts

WordPress Site Inspiration June 7, 2013

View all

G Unpublished posts are shown in Recent Drafts.

Incoming Links

Jessica Neuman Beck linked here saying, "Oh, Theme Customizer with Live Preview, where have ..." on August 24, 2012

H Other sites that have recently linked to your WordPress site are shown as Incoming Links.

Plugins

Most Popular
Contact Form (Install)
Add Contact Form to your WordPress website.

Newest Plugins
Cielo WooCommerce (Install)
Adds Brazilian payment gateway Cielo to WooCommerce

I The Plugins Dashboard widget.

WordPress Blog

Ten Good Years May 31, 2013
It's been ten years since we started this thing, and what a long way we've come. From a discussion between myself and Mike Little about forking our favorite blogging software, to powering 18% of the web. It's been a crazy, exciting, journey, and one that won't stop any time soon. At ten years, it's fun [...] [...]

The Next 10 Starts Now May 27, 2013
All around the globe today, people are celebrating the 10th anniversary of the first WordPress release, affectionately known as #wp10. Watching the feed of photos, tweets, and posts from Auckland to Zambia is incredible; from first-time bloggers to successful WordPress-based business owners, people are coming out in droves to raise a glass and share the [...] [...]

J The WordPress Development Blog shows updates from the people developing WordPress.

Other WordPress News

WPTavern: Pretty WordPress Template Hierarchy Diagram

WPTavern: How To Adopt A Plugin Or Put It Up For Adoption

WordPress.tv: David Jenyns: WordPress and Video SEO

WordPress.tv: Warren Denley: WordPress 101

Lorelle on WP: Help Spread the Word – Writing for the Web Class

K Other WordPress News.

- If you have saved any unpublished posts, you will see them in the Recent Drafts section **G**.

- When other sites link to you, the Incoming Links module will notify you **H**.

- Recently released WordPress plug-ins are listed in the Plugins section **I**.

- The WordPress Developers Blog posts can be accessed through the WordPress Development Blog dashboard widget **J**.

- The Other WordPress News module is similar to the WordPress Development Blog module, but it provides links to articles about WordPress on other popular sites such as www.wordpress.tv **K**.

TIP Want to customize what you see on your Dashboard overview page? It's easy: Just click the Screen Options tab at the top of your screen and choose which modules to show as well as how many columns you'd like **L**. You can also rearrange Dashboard modules by dragging and dropping them into exactly the configuration you want **M**.

Show on screen

☑ Right Now ☑ Recent Comments ☑ Incoming Links ☑ Plugins ☑ Site Stats ☑ QuickPress ☑ Recent Drafts ☑ WordPress Development Blog ☑ Other WordPress News

☑ Welcome

Screen Layout

Number of Columns: ◯ 1 ⦿ 2 ◯ 3 ◯ 4

Screen Options ▲

L Click the Screen Options tab to configure the Dashboard Overview.

Show on screen

☑ Right Now ☑ Recent Comments ☑ Incoming Links ☑ Plugins ☐ Site Stats ☑ QuickPress ☑ Recent Drafts ☑ WordPress Development Blog ☑ Other WordPress News ☐ Welcome

Screen Layout

Number of Columns: ◯ 1 ⦿ 2 ◯ 3 ◯ 4

Screen Options ▲

🏠 Dashboard

Right Now

Content		Discussion	
33	Posts	10	Comments
11	Pages	10	Approved
8	Categories	0	Pending
64	Tags	0	Spam

Theme **Our Theme** with **3 Widgets**

You are using **WordPress 3.6-beta3-24398**.

Akismet has protected your site from 96,991 spam comments already. There's nothing in your spam queue at the moment.

QuickPress

Enter title here

📎 Add Media

Tags (separate with commas)

Save Draft   Reset   **Publish**

Recent Drafts

M Use Drag & Drop Dashboard widgets to customize your screen.

To use the Admin Bar:

1. Log in to your WordPress account and navigate to the front page of your site. An easy way to do this is to click your site's name at the very top of the Admin screen.

2. At the top of your site you will see a dark gray bar with your site's name on the left, your username and icon on the right, and some menu options between **N**. The menu options change depending on which page you're on and the options available to your account level **O**.

   The Admin Bar is not visible to anyone who is not logged in to your site. In other words, your visitors will never see this toolbar.

continues on next page

N The Admin Bar provides quick access to some of the most useful features of your site.

O Different options are available depending on what page you're on.

3. Hover your mouse over a menu item to see the actions that are available to you. For example, if you hover over your name, you will see quick links to edit your profile, access your Dashboard, or log out .

TIP If you want to disable the Dashboard Toolbar entirely, go to Your Profile and deselect the option for Show Toolbar Q.

P Hover over menu items to reveal more options.

Q Disabling the Admin Bar in Your Profile.

Using the Help Tab

Any time you run into a snag in your WordPress Dashboard, the first place to look for answers is the Help tab at the top of your screen. WordPress uses *contextual help*, which means that each Help screen shows information relevant to the section of the Dashboard currently being viewed. The information can include instructions, tips, and links to external resources **R**. Some plug-ins utilize this functionality as well, so it's worthwhile to check the Help tab no matter which screen you're on.

R Contextual help is like a mini WordPress manual right at your fingertips.

Using Feature Pointers

When new features are introduced to WordPress, you will be notified with a Feature Pointer **S**. You can dismiss Feature Pointers by clicking the Dismiss link at the lower right.

S Feature Pointers appear to draw your attention to new WordPress features.

A Even though you haven't yet added content to your site, WordPress supplies some default content to get you started. The "Hello World!" post includes a sample comment so you can see how your site will look once visitors start to interact with it.

B The Sample Page gives you some formatting examples and some basic advice for setting up an About page.

Default Content

When you install WordPress, your site is automatically populated with some default content to get you started **A**. You'll want to delete this default content before publishing your site. Luckily, it's easy: Delete the default post, and the default comment will disappear as well.

You new site also will contain a Sample Page **B**, which offers some formatting examples. You can easily delete this page as well.

To delete the Hello World post:

1. Go to your Dashboard, and find the Right Now widget.
2. Click Post to open the Posts screen **C**.
3. Hover over the "Hello world!" post to view your available actions **D**.
4. Click the Trash link to delete the post.

To delete the Sample Page:

1. Go to your Dashboard, and find the Right Now widget.
2. Click Page to open the Pages screen.
3. Hover over the page titled Sample Page to view your available actions **E**.
4. Click the Trash link to delete the page.

Right Now	
Content	Discussion
1 Post	1 Comment
1 Page	1 Approved
1 Category	0 Pending
0 Tags	0 Spam

C Click Post to open the screen that shows all of your posts.

	Title	Author	Categories	Tags	💬	Date
☐	**Hello world!** Edit I Quick Edit I Trash I View	Admin	Uncategorized	—	**1**	19 hours ago Published

D When you hover over a post's title, you will see a quick list of available actions.

		Author		💬	Date
☐	**Sample Page** Edit I Quick Edit I Trash I View	Admin		**0**	20 hours ago Published

E Just like posts, pages also have a hover menu of available actions.

Upgrading WordPress

Each time WordPress releases an update to the core files, it includes bug fixes, security patches, and improvements to the platform. To get the most out of your WordPress experience, you'll want to be sure you're always running the most up-to-date version.

WordPress makes it easy to update using the automatic update feature introduced in version 2.7. You can also manually update via FTP.

To do an automatic update:

1. When a new version of WordPress is released, you will see a notification at the top of your WordPress Dashboard. Click Please Update Now to get started **A**.

   As a reminder, be sure to always back up your site and files before making any changes to the core! See Chapter 16, "Best Practices," for backup instructions.

2. On the first update screen, click Update Now to start the update process **B**.

continues on next page

Click here to update to a new version of WordPress

WordPress 3.5.1 is available! Please update now.

A The automatic update notice appears at the top of every screen in your Dashboard.

WordPress Updates   Help ▼

Last checked on June 7, 2013 at 8:02 am.   Check Again

Important: before updating, please back up your database and files. For help with updates, visit the Updating WordPress Codex page.

An updated version of WordPress is available.

You can update to WordPress 3.5.1 automatically or download the package and install it manually:

Update Now   Download 3.5.1

While your site is being updated, it will be in maintenance mode. As soon as your updates are complete, your site will return to normal.

B Click Update Now.

3. If your server has sufficient permissions set, the update will begin immediately and you can skip ahead to step 5. Otherwise you will need to supply FTP credentials to proceed.

4. Enter the same FTP information that your hosting company provided for you to use with an FTP client . Click Proceed.

5. When the update is complete, you will automatically be redirected to the WordPress Welcome screen, which shows an overview of what's new **D**.

   Check your site to make sure everything is functioning correctly after the update. If you run into any problems, take a look at Appendix A, "Troubleshooting," at the end of this book.

To update via FTP:

1. In your browser, go to www.wordpress.org/download and click the Download WordPress button on the right of the screen **E**. A compressed file containing the latest version of WordPress will download to your computer.

C You may need to supply your FTP credentials to allow WordPress to add the updated files to the server.

D The update is complete.

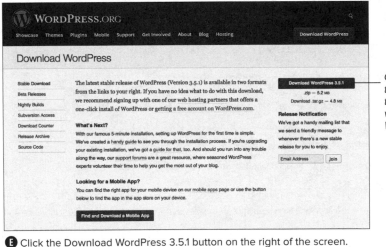

Click here to download the latest version of WordPress

E Click the Download WordPress 3.5.1 button on the right of the screen.

2. Extract the wordpress directory from the ZIP archive by double-clicking the file on your computer **F**.

3. Open your favorite FTP client, enter the settings provided to you by your hosting company, and sign in. You should see a list of files and directories on your local computer as well as on your Web server. Navigate to the wordpress directory on your local computer; then navigate to the directory where you installed WordPress on your server **G**.

continues on next page

Name	Date Modified	Size	Kind
wordpress-3.5.1.zip	Today 4:44 PM	5.4 MB	ZIP archive

F Extract the wordpress directory by double-clicking the file.

Name ▲	Size	Date
.DS_Store	8 KB	Friday, June 7, 2013 1:09 AM
wordpress	--	Jan 24, 2013 7:53 PM
wordpress-3.5.1.zip	5.4 MB	Jun 7, 2013 12:34 AM

Name ▲	Size	Date
cgi-bin	--	6/7/13
index.php	395 B	1/8/12
license.txt	20 KB	5/6/12
readme.html	9 KB	6/7/13
wp-activate.php	5 KB	11/17/12
wp-admin	--	12/11/12
wp-blog-header.php	271 B	1/8/12
wp-comments-post.php	4 KB	4/10/12
wp-config-sample.php	3 KB	11/1/10
wp-config.php	4 KB	6/7/13
wp-content	--	6/7/13
wp-cron.php	3 KB	9/23/12
wp-includes	--	12/11/12
wp-links-opml.php	2 KB	10/23/10
wp-load.php	2 KB	10/26/11
wp-login.php	29 KB	11/30/12
wp-mail.php	8 KB	9/24/12
wp-settings.php	10 KB	11/22/12
wp-signup.php	18 KB	9/11/12
wp-trackback.php	4 KB	1/8/12
xmlrpc.php	3 KB	9/11/12

G Navigate to the directory in which you installed WordPress on your Web server.

4. Select all of the files in the wordpress directory on your local computer, and drag them to the server. You will be asked if you want to replace the files on your server with the ones you're uploading. Select the Apply To All box in your FTP client to apply your choice to all files, and click Replace ⓗ. This will allow the newer files to overwrite your old WordPress installation with the new version. It will not overwrite your user-generated content.

5. When all the new files are uploaded, log in to WordPress in your browser to continue the update process ⓘ.

ⓗ Replace the old files.

ⓘ Log in to WordPress.

6. You'll see the Database Update Required screen. Click Update WordPress Database to continue .

7. When you see Update Complete, click Continue.

8. You'll be taken to the new WordPress Dashboard ⓚ. WordPress has been updated.

   Check your site to make sure that everything is still working. If you have any trouble, take a look at Appendix A.

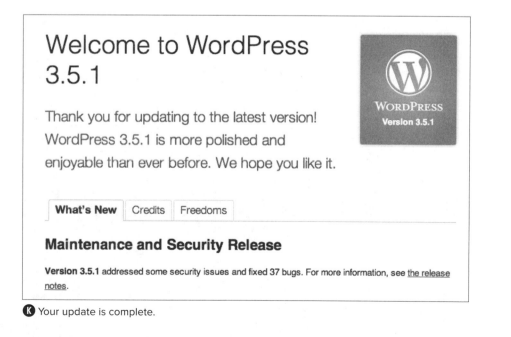

Ⓦ WORDPRESS

Database Update Required

WordPress has been updated! Before we send you on your way, we have to update your database to the newest version.

The update process may take a little while, so please be patient.

Update WordPress Database

Ⓙ Click Update WordPress Database.

Welcome to WordPress 3.5.1

Thank you for updating to the latest version! WordPress 3.5.1 is more polished and enjoyable than ever before. We hope you like it.

Ⓦ WORDPRESS
Version 3.5.1

| **What's New** | Credits | Freedoms |

Maintenance and Security Release

Version 3.5.1 addressed some security issues and fixed 37 bugs. For more information, see the release notes.

Ⓚ Your update is complete.

Putting It All Together

1. **Set up the Dashboard options for your account.** Which modules are you displaying? How do you change the modules that display and the number of columns?

2. **Try out the admin bar.** Can you create a post from there? If you use the search form on the top right, what sort of results will you see?

3. **Update WordPress.** How do you know if you are running the latest version of WordPress?

Settings

One of the great things about WordPress is the way it can be customized. Without entering a smidgeon of code, you can choose how many posts are displayed, pick a static page for your front page, add or change your site's title and tagline, and set sizes for your uploaded images and thumbnails.

You can access all the settings for your WordPress site through the Dashboard's sidebar menu, under Settings.

In This Chapter

General Settings

How Settings Affect Your Site

Unlike Posts or Pages, most of the Settings options affect your site in ways your viewers can't see. Using Settings, you can configure your site in many ways to make it more readable, better looking, and easier to navigate.

The Settings submenu shows all the available configuration options for your site **A**. Some plug-ins add their own configuration options to the Settings section as well **B**.

Settings
General
Writing
Reading
Discussion
Media
Permalinks

A The default WordPress Settings menu.

Settings
General
Writing
Reading
Discussion
Media
Permalinks
WP Super Cache
Sharing

B When you install certain plug-ins, their configuration options will appear in the Settings menu as well.

The General Settings section contains a selection of basic information about your site and how it is configured **C**.

To use General Settings:

1. Set your site title. This is the title that will appear at the top of your browser window; most themes also display this title in the header of the site.

2. Enter a tagline. This is often displayed at the top of the browser window on the homepage of the site. Some themes display the tagline below the site title.

3. If your WordPress installation files are kept separate from your main site, enter the WordPress address and site address; otherwise these fields will automatically be populated with the default URL for your site. Unless you are keeping your WordPress installation files in a separate directory from your actual site, you probably won't need to change these.

	Help ▾

General Settings

Site Title	WordPress Visual Quickstart Guide
Tagline	Demo site
	In a few words, explain what this site is about.
WordPress Address (URL)	http://demo.wpvisualquickstart.com
Site Address (URL)	http://demo.wpvisualquickstart.com
	Enter the address here if you want your site homepage to be different from the directory you installed WordPress.
E-mail Address	author@wpvisualquickstart.com
	This address is used for admin purposes, like new user notification.

C The top half of the General Settings screen, where you can customize your site title, tagline, URL information, and email address.

4. Enter the email address you want WordPress to use when it notifies you of things that require your attention, such as new users and comments that need moderation. The email address you enter here is never displayed on your site.

5. If you want to allow your site's visitors to register on your site, select the Anyone Can Register check box **D**.

continues on next page

Membership	☐ Anyone can register
New User Default Role	Subscriber ⬍
Timezone	UTC+0 ⬍ *UTC time is* `2013-06-18 15:46:50`
	Choose a city in the same timezone as you.
Date Format	⦿ June 18, 2013
	○ 2013/06/18
	○ 06/18/2013
	○ 18/06/2013
	○ Custom: `F j, Y` June 18, 2013
	Documentation on date and time formatting.
Time Format	⦿ 3:46 pm
	○ 3:46 PM
	○ 15:46
	○ Custom: `g:i a` 3:46 pm
Week Starts On	Monday ⬍
Save Changes	

D The lower half of the General Settings screen, where you can customize membership and subscriber options and set your time and date format.

6. Choose the default role for new users (including those you register yourself from the Users link in the Dashboard sidebar). By default, this role is set to Subscriber, but you can choose a new default of Author, Editor, or even Administrator. User roles are explained more fully in Chapter 4, "Managing Accounts." Be careful when you change the default role, especially if you have the Membership check box set to allow anyone to register.

7. Set your time zone to make sure the timestamp on your posts is accurate and scheduled posts are published when you expect them to be. You can choose UTC variants or find a city in the drop-down that's in your time zone. If you'd like WordPress to automatically account for daylight savings, choosing a city is the way to go **E**.

8. Select the format in which you'd like the dates to appear on your site. You can select from the preselected options or choose custom formatting rules. WordPress uses the same settings for custom date strings that are used in the `date()` function in PHP.

9. You can customize the way WordPress processes times by adjusting the Time Format setting.

10. Choose the day on which you'd like your week to start when WordPress displays calendars marking your updates.

Los Angeles ⬍	*UTC time is 2013-06-17 20:38:50*	*Local time is 2013-06-17 13:38:50*

Choose a city in the same timezone as you.

This timezone is currently in daylight saving time.
Standard time begins on: November 3, 2013 2:00 am .

E Choose a city that shares your time zone and WordPress will automatically adjust for daylight savings time.

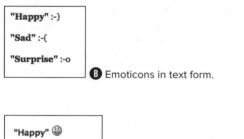

A Configure your writing settings here.

"Happy" :-)

"Sad" :-(

"Surprise" :-o

B Emoticons in text form.

"Happy" 😊

"Sad" 😞

"Surprise" 😮

C WordPress can convert text emoticons into graphics in your posts.

Writing Settings

The Writing Settings section is used to configure how content, such as blog posts, displays on your site A. You can also set up your remote publishing settings here.

To configure your writing settings:

1. If you would like WordPress to convert text emoticons B to graphics C, make that selection here. You may also choose to have WordPress automatically correct invalidly nested XHTML. If you regularly use the Visual Editor when you're entering posts, it's a good idea to enable this feature—but be aware that some plug-ins don't work correctly with this feature turned on.

   Plug-ins that filter the post content or rely on specific markup or short codes may not behave normally because WordPress may convert the code that they rely on into valid XHTML.

continues on next page

2. If you've already created some post categories (see Chapter 7, "Adding Content," for instructions on setting up post categories), you can choose the category you'd like to use by default.

3. If you'd like your default post format to be something other than a standard post, choose the post format here. Note that in order to see this option, your theme must be set up to use post formats. For more on using post formats, see Chapter 7, "Adding Content."

Update Services

At the very bottom of the Writing Settings you'll see a text box where you can enter the URLs for site update services—but what are they, and why would you use them?

Site update services like Ping-o-Matic notify a number of different services each time you update your blog. Such services can potentially drive traffic to your site.

WordPress has a list of XML-RPC Ping Services on the codex at http://codex.wordpress.org/Update_Services. Bear in mind, though, that pinging a lot of services every time you post can slow down your site.

If you want to disable this feature, just delete all the URLs from the Update Services section of your site.

Posting from Outside of WordPress

With WordPress it's possible to use a variety of tools to add new posts to your site.

1. Press This is a *bookmarklet*, a special link that you can use to quickly add a post while browsing the Internet. Drag the Press This link to your bookmark bar, and then click it when you find content you'd like to share on your blog. A window will pop up with an automatically formatted link to your content as well as options to add images, text, and other elements to your new post **D**.

2. Post Via E-mail lets you email updates to your blog. To set this up, you'll need to know the server settings for the POP3 email account you've established expressly for the purpose of making WordPress posts **E**. We talk about this in much more detail in Chapter 7, "Adding Content."

D Clicking the Press This bookmarklet lets you quickly post right from your browser.

E Set up POP3 access to post by email.

Reading Settings

The Reading Settings section allows you to control aspects of how WordPress displays your content **A**. Set the tone for your site by choosing whether you want your front page to display your most recent blog posts or a static page, if you don't want visitors jumping straight into your posts. You can also set the number of posts per page and customize your feed settings here.

To set your reading preferences:

1. Choose whether your front page displays your latest posts (blog format) or a static page.

2. If you choose a static page, the first thing you will need to do is create two pages in the Pages section of the WordPress admin: one called Home—which will contain the content for your new static home page—and one that will display your blog posts (you can call it Blog or News or anything you prefer).

   Leave the posts page blank; just create the page in the Pages section of the WordPress admin and publish it.

A Customize your display settings here. You can choose how your site looks to visitors and how your feed appears to people using a feed reader.

Front page displays	○ Your latest posts
	⦿ A static page (select below)
	Front page: Home ⇳
	Posts page: Blog ⇳

B Once you have created pages for your front page and your posts, you can choose them from the Front Page Displays section of Reading Settings.

3. If you are using a static home page, navigate back to Reading Settings and choose your new Front page and Posts page from the drop-down menus **B**.

4. Choose the number of posts you want your blog pages to display. The default is 10, but you can choose any number you'd like. Keep in mind that if you display a large number of posts at once, your site may load very slowly.

   If you have more posts than you are loading at any one time, they will be accessible to your site viewers via forward and back links.

5. Choose the number of posts available to new subscribers to your RSS feed by changing the number of items under "Syndication feeds show the most recent."

6. Set whether people viewing your posts through a feed reader like Feedly can see the full text of your posts or a summary that includes a link to your site.

7. Choose whether to display your site in search engine results. If your site isn't ready for primetime, you can check this box to discourage search engines from indexing it. Just remember to disable this feature when you're ready to share with the world!

Discussion Settings

Correctly configured discussion settings can save you a lot of administrative headaches. The Discussion Settings section controls how you handle comments on your blog, from global preferences to avatar display **A**. You can also help prevent spam by using comment moderation or blacklisting keywords.

To set comment controls:

1. Under Default Article Settings, choose how you want to handle comments, pingbacks, and trackbacks. If you want to disable commenting on your site entirely, you may do so here by deselecting the check box next to "Allow people to post comments on new articles." To disable commenting on an individual post without turning it off for the whole site, see Chapter 10, "Managing Comments."

A Preferences set here give you control over who can interact with your site and how they can do it.

2. If comments are enabled, choose whether or not to restrict commenting to logged-in users or users who have filled out their name and email address on your contact form. You can also opt to automatically turn off commenting on older articles. Also, you can control the way your comments display: nesting, pagination, and sort order are all options here.

3. Choose whether you are notified every time you get a new comment or when a comment is held for moderation. If you choose not to be notified when a comment is held for moderation, you will see the comment in the moderation queue the next time you log in to your WordPress Dashboard.

4. Choose whether comments must always be approved or whether comment authors must have a previously approved comment in order for new comments to automatically appear.

5. Set the number of links in a single comment that will trigger moderation. You can also add keywords to the Comment Moderation settings box to have any comment containing those words automatically held for moderation. For more about comment moderation, see Chapter 10, "Managing Comments."

6. If there are words, phrases, or IP addresses you know are spam, you can enter them here under Comment Blacklist. Comments with any content matching blacklisted terms will automatically be marked as spam.

continues on next page

7. Choose the avatar options for your users **B**. You can disable avatars entirely under Avatar Display, but if you choose to display them you can set a Maximum Rating and choose the default avatar for those who don't have Gravatars or custom avatars. The options that are marked as "Generated" will show a random avatar in your chosen style for all users who do not have their own.

TIP If you installed the Jetpack plug-in, you can choose to enable Gravatar Hovercards, which show a larger avatar photo and a quick blurb about your site's authors and commenters **C**. Learn more about the Jetpack plug-in in Chapter 15, "More Ways to Customize WordPress."

C Jetpack users can enable Gravatar Hovercards that link back to each user's Gravatar profile.

Avatars

An avatar is an image that follows you from weblog to weblog appearing beside your name when you comment on avatar enabled sites. Here you can enable the display of avatars for people who comment on your site.

Avatar Display	☑ Show Avatars
Maximum Rating	◉ G — Suitable for all audiences
	○ PG — Possibly offensive, usually for audiences 13 and above
	○ R — Intended for adult audiences above 17
	○ X — Even more mature than above
Default Avatar	For users without a custom avatar of their own, you can either display a generic logo or a generated one based on their e-mail address.
	◉ Mystery Man
	○ Blank
	○ Gravatar Logo
	○ Identicon (Generated)
	○ Wavatar (Generated)
	○ MonsterID (Generated)
	○ Retro (Generated)

Save Changes

B If you display avatars for commenters and users of your site, you can choose what shows up when someone hasn't specified their own image.

Media Settings

The Media Settings section controls how your images and embedded content display on your site Ⓐ. Images inserted into the body of a post or page using the Media Uploader will automatically be created in the dimensions you set here. You can also specify how your Media Library files are organized.

continues on next page

Ⓐ Set preferences for your media display under Media Settings.

To specify media settings:

1. Choose a thumbnail size. You can choose to crop your thumbnail to the exact dimensions you specify here; otherwise the thumbnail image will be proportionate, with the image reduced until the longest side equals your width or height.

2. Choose a Medium size for your images. This size is often used in the body of blog posts or pages.

3. Set a Large size for your images. This is the size usually used for full-page image posts or lightbox (pop-in) enlargements.

4. Choose whether to organize your files into month- and year-based folders.

Permalinks

The Permalink Settings are used to control the way that WordPress builds URLs to your pages and blog posts **Ⓐ**.

The default setting uses yoursite.com/?p=123, where *123* is a numeric identifier for your content. However, there are good reasons to change to an alternate permalink structure. "Pretty" permalinks (links that have a contextual, readable word list rather than a string of characters) are both more informative to humans looking at the URL and more readable by search engines that crawl your site.

To set up custom permalinks:

1. Choose one of the common settings under Permalink Settings or enter your own custom structure. WordPress developers recommend using a numeric base (such as a year or date) for speed of retrieval from the database. If you're a casual user this shouldn't be an issue, but power users with thousands of posts may notice a speed increase by utilizing a numeric base.

2. In the Optional section, choose whether you want to enable a category or tag base. For example, if you choose *ideas* as a category base, your category links would appear like this: yoursite.com/ideas/uncategorized.

Permalink Settings

By default WordPress uses web URLs which have question marks and lots of numbers in them, however WordPress offers you the ability to create a custom URL structure for your permalinks and archives. This can improve the aesthetics, usability, and forward-compatibility of your links. A number of tags are available, and here are some examples to get you started.

Common Settings

◉ Default   `http://demo.wpvisualquickstart.com/?p=123`

○ Day and name   `http://demo.wpvisualquickstart.com/2013/06/18/sample-post/`

○ Month and name   `http://demo.wpvisualquickstart.com/2013/06/sample-post/`

○ Numeric   `http://demo.wpvisualquickstart.com/archives/123`

○ Post name   `http://demo.wpvisualquickstart.com/sample-post/`

○ Custom Structure   `http://demo.wpvisualquickstart.com` [_____]

Optional

If you like, you may enter custom structures for your category and tag URLs here. For example, using `topics` as your category base would make your category links like `http://example.org/topics/uncategorized/` . If you leave these blank the defaults will be used.

Category base [_____]

Tag base [_____]

[Save Changes]

Ⓐ Choose the way your permalinks appear.

Putting It All Together

1. See how changing options in your WordPress settings modifies what is displayed on the front end of your site. Try changing the tagline and site title. Where do the new values appear?

2. **Modify your permalinks.** If you use a date for permalinks, will it also show up for static pages or only on blog posts?

3. **Set up a static front page.** Is there any difference between this page and other static pages on your site?

4. **Experiment with comments.** What notifications do you get when a comment is added to a post?

Managing Accounts

WordPress user accounts allow people to access your site and its content in different ways. Administrators have full access to all parts of your site, including theme and plug-in settings and user management. You can set up Author and Editor accounts to let your users post articles, and Subscriber accounts make commenting a breeze. You can even restrict access to certain portions of your site to registered users.

In this chapter, we'll give you the lowdown on all the account types and how to use them. We'll also show you how to configure your own account to get the most out of your WordPress experience by enabling and disabling such features as the Admin toolbar and the Visual Editor.

In This Chapter

Configuring Your Account

Make your WordPress installation as unique as you are. You can customize everything from the way your name is displayed to the color scheme for your admin screen.

To access your account information:

1. Click your username on the top right of any area in your Admin toolbar (where it says "Howdy, *username*") **A**.

   or

2. Click Users > Your Profile in the sidebar.

A Click your username to edit your account information.

B Profile options in the admin screen.

To set up your profile:

1. From the Profile page, choose among the Personal Options **B**. You can choose to disable the Visual (WYSIWYG) Editor when writing and choose a color scheme for your admin dashboard, plus you can enable keyboard shortcuts for moderating comments. You can also choose whether to display the Admin toolbar when viewing your site.

2. In the Name section of the profile page, change or enter your full name and a nickname, and then choose your preferred display name from the drop-down menu **C**. This name will display in the "Howdy, *username*" salutation at the top of the admin screen and also on your posts and comments.

continues on next page

Name		
Username	admin	Usernames cannot be changed.
First Name	Site	
Last Name	Administrator	
Nickname *(required)*	admin	
Display name publicly as	Site Administrator ▾	

C You can change anything except your username, and you can choose a preferred nickname from the drop-down menu.

3. If you want to provide additional contact information, do so in the Contact Info section. You can change the email address associated with your username, and you can add other contact information, such as the URL for your website and your instant messaging identities **D**.

4. In the About Yourself section, add biographical information if you like. Some themes display this publicly on the site. The About Yourself section is also where you can update your password **E**. You'll use this password to log in to the site, so be sure to choose something you will remember! WordPress will let you know whether your password is strong or weak in the Strength indicator.

TIP When you're choosing a password, WordPress recommends using upper- and lowercase letters, numbers, and symbols (! " ? $ % ^ &) to keep hackers from accessing your account.

Contact Info

E-mail *(required)*	author@wpvisualquickstart.com
Website	
AIM	
Yahoo IM	
Jabber / Google Talk	

D Update your email address and add other contact info here.

About Yourself

Biographical Info	I'm a WordPress designer and developer and author of the WordPress Visual QuickStart Guide for Peachpit Press.
	Share a little biographical information to fill out your profile. This may be shown publicly.
New Password	•••••••••••••• *If you would like to change the password type a new one. Otherwise leave this blank.*
	•••••••••••••• *Type your new password again.*
	Strong *Hint: The password should be at least seven characters long. To make it stronger, use upper and lower case letters, numbers and symbols like ! " ? $ % ^ &).*

Update Profile

E The Strength indicator will tell you whether you have chosen a password that would be difficult for a hacker to guess.

Managing User Accounts

Whether your WordPress site is a solo affair or a group effort, user accounts make it easy to see who has access to what. You can add new user accounts manually or allow prospective users to add themselves (at an account level that you have specified). You can get rid of troublesome or outdated accounts with just a few clicks.

Subscribers vs. Visitors

Anyone on the Internet can visit your site once it is live. If you've enabled commenting, your visitors have the ability to leave comments on your site, which can sometimes be a problem if you get targeted by a spambot or find yourself fielding hostile anonymous messages.

One way to cut down on spam and add a degree of accountability is to require that visitors sign up as subscribers before they can comment. (See the "Discussion Settings" section in Chapter 3, "Settings," for details.) A Subscriber account is a WordPress user type that gives commenters the ability to read your site and to fill out their own profile. Subscribers can comment and edit their own profiles, but they cannot add new content to your site.

Another added bonus of requiring subscriber accounts for commenters: If someone is posting hostile or harassing comments, you can simply delete that person's account. As a visitor the person still can view your posts, but no longer will be able to comment on them.

continues on next page

To add a user account:

1. Click Users in the sidebar menu to access the list of current user accounts for your WordPress site **A**. You'll be taken to the Users page **B**.

2. Click Add New to add a new user. You'll be taken to the Add New User screen **C**.

3. Enter a username, email address, and password for your new user (the user will have the option of changing the password when he or she logs in). You can select whether you want to send login information (including the password you've chosen) to the new user by email.

4. Set the user's first and last name and Web site address here, and select the new user's role from the drop-down menu **D**.

A Click Users to access the list of current user accounts.

B Current users and their roles are listed here.

C The Add New User screen lets you manually add a new user.

D Fill out these fields to create a new user.

5. Click Add User to create the new user account. You'll return to the Users screen, where you'll see a confirmation message at the top of the page **E**.

TIP If you don't select the "Send this password to the new user by email" check box in the Add New User screen, you'll need to notify the user of the login information yourself.

The default user role for new users can be set or changed in Settings > General.

To change user roles:

1. On the Users page, select the check box next to the username of the user whose role you want to change.

2. From the "Change role to" drop-down menu, choose the new role **F**.

3. Click the Change button when you have made your selection to apply the new role to the selected account(s). A message saying "Changed role(s)" will appear at the top of the screen **G**.

The More, The Merrier: Multiple Authors

If you plan to have more than one person writing on your site, you can take advantage of Author accounts. Authors can write, manage, and publish their own posts without being able to edit anyone else's. Each post will be associated with the author's name. You can even set up author profile pages that display each author's bio, a link to their personal web sites, and a list of the articles they have published on your site.

To learn how to create author pages, see Chapter 15, "More Ways to Customize WordPress."

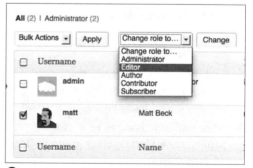

F Choose a user and change roles using the drop-down menu.

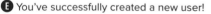

E You've successfully created a new user!

G Success! You've changed a user's role.

Role *changed from Subscriber to Editor*

Breakdown of User Account Types

Account types in WordPress are also referred to as *roles*, and they're broken down as follows:

- Super Admin: When multi-site features are enabled in WordPress, a Super Admin can access the site network administrative features, as well as all other features available to an Administrator (see the section "Administering a Blog Network" in Chapter 14, "One Installation, Multiple Blogs").
- Administrator: This is typically the most privileged account type used for a single site, with access to all administrative features, including theme editing and user management.
- Editor: Editors can publish and manage their own posts and pages as well as those of other Editors, Authors, and Contributors.
- Author: This role gives users the ability to write, manage, and publish their own posts and pages.
- Contributor: A Contributor can write and manage his or her own posts, but cannot publish without approval from an Editor or Administrator.
- Subscriber: This type of user can read and comment on posts and receive notification when new articles are published.

To edit user profiles:

1. On the Users page, click a username to open the user's profile.

   Edit the user's profile. As the admin you can assign user roles in addition to setting general profile information **H**.

2. After making changes to a user's profile, click Update User at the bottom of the screen.

   A confirmation will appear at the top of the page **I**.

H The User Profile editing screen.

I The message User Updated lets you know that your changes have been saved.

	Username	Name
☐	admin	Site Administrator
☑	jessica Edit I Delete	Jessica Beck
☐	matt	Matt Beck

J Choose users to delete from this list.

K Click Apply to continue.

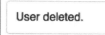

M You'll see a message telling you how many users were deleted.

L Choose an option and confirm deletion.

To delete user accounts:

1. On the Users page, select the check boxes next to the name of the user(s) you wish you delete **J**.

2. From the Bulk Actions drop-down menu, select Delete **K**. Click Apply to go to the Delete Users page.

3. You can either delete all of the posts and links associated with the users you're deleting, or you can assign them to another user, such as the admin account **L**. Click Confirm Deletion.

   Back on the Users page, you'll see a confirmation message at the top of the screen telling you how many users were deleted **M**.

TIP If the user you're deleting has contributed content to your site that you want to keep, you can assign those posts and links to another user. If you're deleting a user because of inappropriate or abusive posts or comments, choosing the Delete All option is best.

Putting It All Together

1. **Experiment with your profile options**. When you enter biographical information, is it displayed on your site?

2. **Create an alternate user account.** When you set up a new user, can you use the same email address you already used for your administrator account?

3. **Experiment with user roles.** Change the alternate user account you created in step 2 to a contributor account. If you log in as that user, how does the Dashboard change? Can you create new posts?

4. **Try to delete the alternate account you created above.** What happens to any posts that you created with that user?

Setting Up a WordPress Theme

One great aspect of WordPress is that you can make your site look pretty much however you want it to using *themes*. Themes are sort of like outfits for your site: They change the way it looks (and to a certain degree how it functions), while the underlying content stays exactly the same.

In this chapter, we'll show you how to activate and use a WordPress default theme, how to choose and activate a new theme, and how to use the Theme Customizer, which allows you to tweak and edit a theme before it goes live on your site. We'll also show you how to add and change custom headers and backgrounds, so your site always looks fresh and new.

Using the WordPress Default Theme

Each year WordPress releases a new default theme, optimized to take advantage of new features introduced into the WordPress core. The theme is automatically added to your theme folder with a fresh WordPress installation or upgrade. These themes are designed to be highly customizable.

Twenty Thirteen is the default WordPress theme for 2013. It's a colorful theme with a responsive layout that is optimized to many different screen sizes (such as monitors, tablets, and smartphones). It incorporates post formats, which give things like image posts or link posts a different look from standard posts. (You can learn more about post formats in Chapter 7, "Adding Content.") The Twenty Thirteen theme includes the option to use a standard sidebar, a large widgetized footer area, or both.

To activate and use Twenty Thirteen:

1. In the left sidebar menu, choose Appearance > Themes to access the Themes screen **A**.

   In the Manage Themes section, your active theme appears at the top, followed by a list of other installed themes.

continues on next page

A The Themes section in the WordPress admin screen shows your active theme as well as any other themes currently available to you.

2. If the Twenty Thirteen theme is not currently the active theme, find it in the list of available themes and click the Activate link **B**.

3. Below the Twenty Thirteen theme description you will see shortcut links to the available theme options. (You can also access these links in the Appearance sidebar menu.) Click Widgets to get started **C**.

B Click the Activate link to activate a new theme.

C Options for the Twenty Thirteen theme are listed below the description and can also be accessed through the Appearance menu in the sidebar. Click Widgets to get started.

D The Twenty Thirteen theme has two widgetized areas.

4. In the Widgets screen, you will see that the Twenty Thirteen theme has two widgetized areas **D**. (For more details about these widgetized areas and what sections of the theme they correspond to, check out the sidebar "Twenty Thirteen Theme Options." To learn more about widgets and how to use them, go to Chapter 6, "Widgets and Plug-ins.") Drag widgets to each section to add them.

5. Next, choose Appearance > Menus to assign a custom menu. If you have no custom menus, a default menu will display **E**. Click Create Menu to save your default menu as a custom menu. After you save your menu, you will see an option to select Menu Settings at the bottom of the menu.

continues on next page

E If you have not yet created a custom menu, you can save your default menu by clicking the Create Menu button.

6. Under Menu Settings, find the section labeled Theme Options and select Navigation Menu to assign this menu to the main navigation of your site. Click Save Menu ⏺. (You'll learn more about creating and managing menus in Chapter 8, "Menus.")

TIP You can make many of these changes and more using the **Theme Customizer** in **Appearance > Customize.** You'll find complete instructions later in this chapter in the "Using the Theme Customizer" section.

| Menu Name | Menu 1 | | Save Menu |

Menu Structure

Drag each item into the order you prefer. Click the arrow on the right of the item to reveal additional configuration options.

Blog	Page ▼
Home	Page ▼
Sample Page	Page ▼

Menu Settings

| *Auto add pages* | ☐ Automatically add new top-level pages to this menu |
| *Theme locations* | ☑ Navigation Menu |

Delete Menu   Save Menu

⏺ Select Navigation Menu under Theme Locations to assign this menu to your theme's main navigation.

Twenty Thirteen Theme Options

The Twenty Thirteen theme has several customizable sections 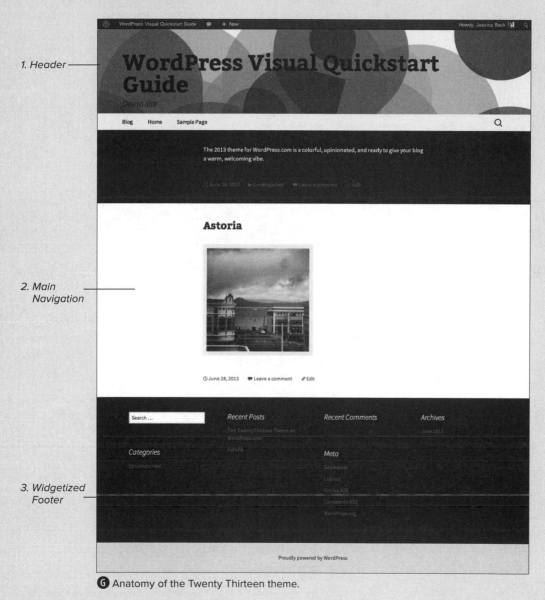. Here's a breakdown of each one and which section of the site it corresponds to:

- Menu: The custom menu you choose in the Menus section will appear at the top of each page on your site, just below the header image.

1. Header

2. Main Navigation

3. Widgetized Footer

G Anatomy of the Twenty Thirteen theme.

- Header: You can choose among several default header images, or you can add your own using the instructions found later in this chapter.
- Widgets: The available widgetized areas are Main Widget Area (located in the theme footer) and the Secondary Widget Area (an optional sidebar that appears to the right of your content) **Ⓗ**.

Sample Page

This is an example page. It's different from a blog post because it will stay in one place and will show up in your site navigation (in most themes). Most people start with an About page that introduces them to potential site visitors. It might say something like this:

Hi there! I'm a bike messenger by day, aspiring actor by night, and this is my blog. I live in Los Angeles, have a great dog named Jack, and I like piña coladas. (And gettin' caught in the rain.)

...or something like this:

The XYZ Doohickey Company was founded in 1971, and has been providing quality doohickeys to the public ever since. Located in Gotham City, XYZ employs over 2,000 people and does all kinds of awesome things for the Gotham community.

As a new WordPress user, you should go to your dashboard to delete this page and create new pages for your content. Have fun!

✎ Edit

Pages

Blog

Home

Sample Page

Recent Posts

The TwentyThirteen Theme on WordPress.com

Astoria

Ⓗ A page using the Twenty Thirteen theme with the optional widgetized sidebar.

Choosing a New Theme

With all the free and premium themes available, it's a breeze to change the look and feel of your WordPress Web site. Your theme dictates the appearance of your site, including the color scheme, typography, background images, and layout. Some themes even add functionality to your site, such as slideshows, Twitter stream integration, or theme-specific widgets.

To add a new theme to your site:

1. Choose Appearance > Themes, and click the Install Themes tab **Ⓐ**.

   The Install Themes screen opens.

continues on next page

Ⓐ Click the Install Themes tab on the Themes screen to add a new theme.

2. Perform a search to find the theme you wish to add. You can search by term, author, or tag. Enter your search term in the text field, and click Search **B**.

You can also use the Feature Filter to assist you with this process simply by checking the boxes that match the features you are looking for **C**. The Feature Filter can help you narrow down your search by only displaying themes that match your selected colors, columns, width, features, and/or subject. After selecting the desired features, click Find Themes.

Search for themes by keyword.

| responsive | ⊗ | Search |

B Search for the theme you want to add to your site.

Feature Filter

Find a theme based on specific features.

Colors

☐ Black	☐ Blue	☐ Brown	☐ Gray	☐ Green
☐ Orange	☐ Pink	☐ Purple	☐ Red	☐ Silver
☐ Tan	☐ White	☐ Yellow	☐ Dark	☐ Light

Columns

| ☐ One Column | ☐ Two Columns | ☐ Three Columns | ☐ Four Columns | ☐ Left Sidebar |
| ☐ Right Sidebar | | | | |

Width

| ☐ Fixed Width | ☐ Flexible Width |

Features

☐ Blavatar	☐ BuddyPress	☐ Custom Background	☐ Custom Colors	☐ Custom Header
☐ Custom Menu	☐ Editor Style	☐ Featured Image Header	☐ Featured Images	☐ Flexible Header
☐ Front Page Posting	☐ Full Width Template	☐ Microformats	☐ Post Formats	☐ RTL Language Support
☐ Sticky Post	☐ Theme Options	☐ Threaded Comments	☐ Translation Ready	

Subject

| ☐ Holiday | ☐ Photoblogging | ☐ Seasonal |

| Find Themes |

C Use the Feature Filter to narrow down your results.

3. In the list of search results, find the theme you wish to install. Click the Preview link to see a preview of the theme; once you've decided on a theme, click Install 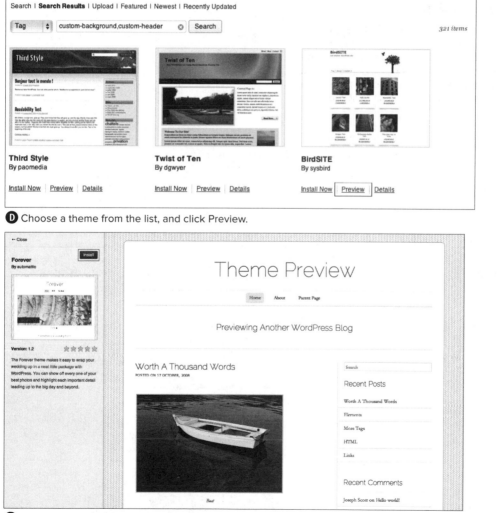.

4. Wait for the message *Successfully installed the theme* to appear. This lets you know that WordPress has completed downloading and unzipping the theme files 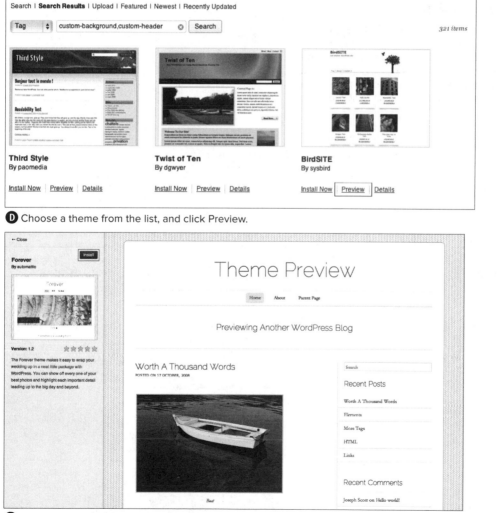.

continues on next page

 Choose a theme from the list, and click Preview.

 Click Install to install your chosen theme.

5. If you want to activate the theme right away, click Activate.

You will be taken to the Themes screen, and you will see a confirmation message at the top of the screen **F**. The theme will immediately be live on your site.

TIP You can activate any theme that has been installed on your site by choosing **Appearance > Themes. Select the theme you want in your list of Available Themes, and click the Activate link G.**

TIP Want to upload a theme that isn't in the WordPress theme repository? Simply download the theme to your computer, and then upload the ZIP file by navigating to the Install Themes screen as described earlier and choosing Upload from the links at the top of the screen **H**.

Installing Theme: Forever 1.2

Downloading install package from http://wordpress.org/themes/download/forever.1.2.zip...

Unpacking the package...

Installing the theme...

Successfully installed the theme **Forever 1.2**.

Live Preview | Activate | Return to Theme Installer

F Success! Your new theme has been installed. Click Activate to apply it to your site.

New theme activated. Visit site

Forever

Current Theme
Forever

By Automattic | Version 1.2

The Forever theme makes it easy to wrap your wedding up in a neat little package with WordPress. You can show off every one of your best photos and highlight each important detail leading up to the big day and beyond.

Customize   OPTIONS: Widgets | Menus | Theme Options | Header | Background

G The confirmation message at the top of the screen lets you know your new theme has been activated.

Search | Upload | Featured | Newest | Recently Updated

Install a theme in .zip format

If you have a theme in a .zip format, you may install it by uploading it here.

Choose File | no file selected   Install Now

H Upload a new theme in ZIP file format by choosing the Upload link.

![Twenty Thirteen theme preview]

Twenty Thirteen
By the WordPress team

Activate | Live Preview | Details   Delete

Ⓐ Click the Live Preview link to open the Theme Customizer.

Using the Theme Customizer

Want to customize that theme before you commit to activating it on your site? The Theme Customizer is the place to do it. Here you can make changes to the look and feel of any installed theme and preview the results without altering the way your site appears to visitors. When you're happy with your changes, you can publish your new theme with one click.

To use the Theme Customizer:

1. Go to the main Themes menu by clicking Appearance > Themes. In your list of available themes, choose the Live Preview link Ⓐ.

2. A preview of your theme will open. Notice the available theme customization options on the left Ⓑ.

continues on next page

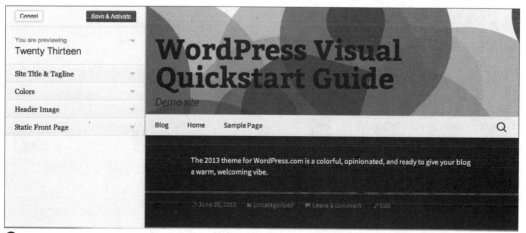

Ⓑ The Theme Customizer shows available theme options on the left and a live preview of the new theme applied to your site on the right. Any changes you make in the options section will immediately display in the live preview area.

3. Click the Site Title & Tagline heading to expand the section **C**. You can change the text that displays here or choose not to show it at all.

4. Click the Colors heading. Any colors in the theme that can be modified will show here **D**. Click the Select Color button to view the color picker, which allows you to select a new color by entering a hexadecimal code at the top or by clicking anywhere inside the rainbow graphic to find the exact color you want **E**.

Site Title & Tagline

Site Title

WordPress Visual Quickstart Guide

Tagline

Demo site

☑ Display Header Text

C Edit your site title and tagline, or hide them altogether by clearing the Display Header Text check box.

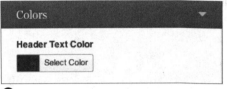

D Any site colors you can customize will show here.

Colors

Header Text Color

| Current Color | #220e10 | Default |

◀ Collapse

E Click anywhere in the color picker to choose a new color, or enter the hexadecimal code for the color you want.

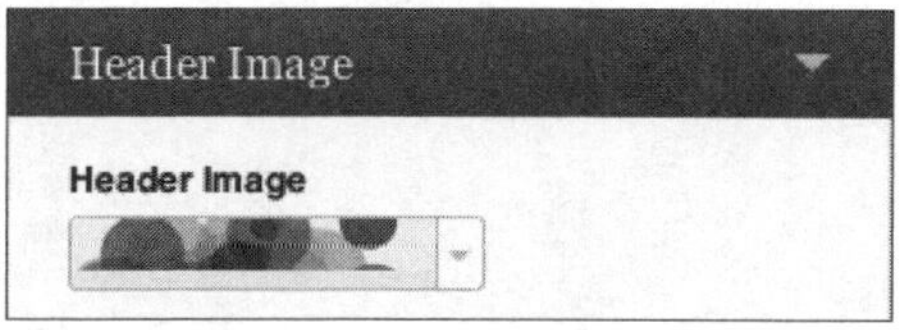

![Header Image dialog showing the theme's header image]

F The theme's header image shows here. Click to view all available header images.

![Header Image dialog showing available header images with Default option and Remove Image button]

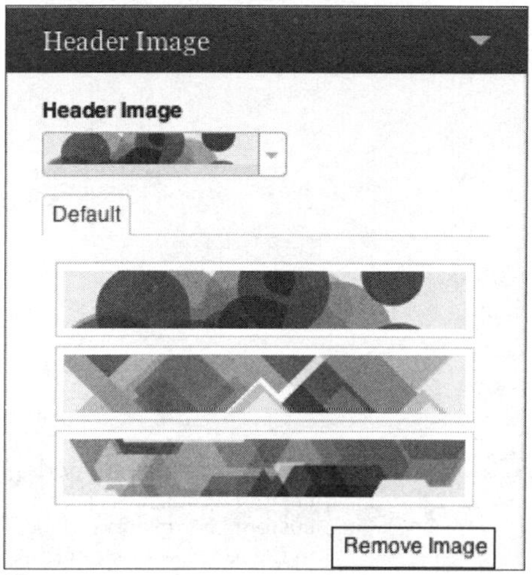

G You can choose a new header image or click Remove Image to get rid of the header image entirely.

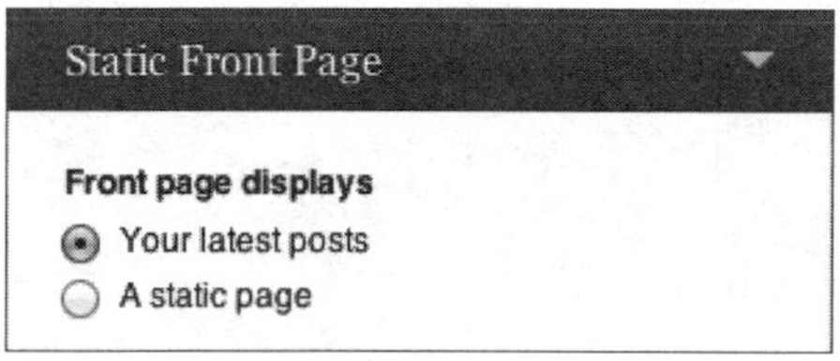

![Static Front Page dialog with Front page displays options]

H Choose whether to show your latest posts or a static front page to your site's visitors.

I Click Save & Activate to make your customized theme live on your site.

5. Click the Header Image heading. The currently selected header image shows here **F**. Click the triangle graphic next to the current header image to view all the available header images. You can select one by clicking it, or you can disable the header image altogether by clicking Remove Image **G**.

6. Click the Static Front Page heading. Choose whether to display your latest posts or a static page as the front page of your site **H**.

7. When you are happy with your changes, click Save & Activate to make the theme live on your site **I**. If you'd rather exit without applying the new theme, click Cancel.

Custom Headers and Backgrounds

Customization options vary from theme to theme. Two common extras are custom headers and custom backgrounds. If your theme supports these, you will see links to Header and Background customization sections in the Options area below your theme's description 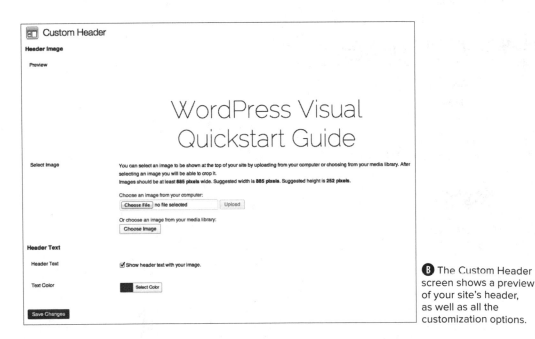.

To add a custom header:

1. Click the Header link in the Options area to open the Custom Header screen Ⓑ.

Ⓐ If your theme supports custom headers and custom backgrounds, links to these will appear in the Options section.

Ⓑ The Custom Header screen shows a preview of your site's header, as well as all the customization options.

2. Upload an image from your computer, or select it from your Media Library **C**.

3. The Crop screen will open **D**. Select the portion of your image to use as your site header, and click the Crop And Publish button.

continues on next page

Select Image	You can select an image to be shown at the top of your site by uploading from your computer or choosing from your media library. After selecting an image you will be able to crop it. Images should be at least **885 pixels** wide. Suggested width is **885 pixels**. Suggested height is **252 pixels**. Choose an image from your computer: [**Choose File**] no file selected [Upload] Or choose an image from your media library: [Choose Image]

C Upload a new header image, or choose one from the Media Library.

Crop Header Image

Choose the part of the image you want to use as your header.

[Crop and Publish]

D Crop your header image to fit into the allotted space.

4. Your new header image will preview on the Custom Header screen ⓔ. If you're not happy with the preview, you can follow the steps above to upload a new image. You can also choose from any of your previously uploaded and cropped header images or choose not to display a header image at all ⓕ.

5. Choose whether to show header text and change the color of your header text in the Header Text section ⓖ.

6. When you are happy with your custom header, click Save Changes to display the new header on your site.

ⓔ A preview of your new header image will display on the Custom Header page.

ⓕ Choose any previously uploaded header image or disable the header image entirely here.

ⓖ Use the toggle to display or hide your header text and change the color here.

ⓗ The Custom Background screen shows your current background image as well as your available customization options.

ⓘ Upload a new background image, or choose one from the Media Library.

ⓙ Choose the display options for your new background image here.

To add a custom background:

1. Click the Background link in the Options area to open the Custom Background screen **ⓗ**. A preview of your current background image will show. If you don't want to use a background image at all, click the Remove Background Image button.

2. Upload a new background image from your computer, or choose it from your Media Library **ⓘ**.

3. Choose the display options for your new background image **ⓙ**. You can set your background position, choose whether or not to tile the image, and set whether the background remains in a fixed position or scrolls with your content. If your background image has transparent or semi-transparent pixels, you can also set a background color.

4. When you are happy with your new background image, click Save Changes to publish it on your site **ⓚ**.

TIP You can also access Header and Background customization areas in the Appearance menu for your active theme or through the Live Preview section of a theme that has not yet been activated.

ⓚ A theme with a custom header and custom background enabled.

Putting It All Together

1. **Customize the Twenty Thirteen theme.** How do you set up the widgetized footer? Can you modify the header?

2. **Find a new theme.** Use the Feature Filter to locate a theme with four columns. How many themes did you find? How do you preview a theme?

3. **Activate a new theme.** Install a new theme from the Install Themes screen and activate it. How else can you activate a theme?

4. **Use the Theme Customizer to make changes to your theme.** What information is editable from here?

5. **Update your theme's background image.** How do the various display options affect your site's background?

Widgets and Plug-ins

Want to add some extra functionality to your site? Widgets and plug-ins are the answer. Widgets and plug-ins extend the functionality of WordPress, allowing you to easily add extra features and enhanced customization options, which could be anything from simple contact forms to complex online e-commerce solutions.

Because plug-ins and widgets are installed separately from your theme, you usually won't need to add any code to your template files to get them to work.

In this chapter, we'll tell you about the difference between widgets and plug-ins, explain how to manage them and use them on your site, and give you an overview of some popular plug-ins.

In This Chapter

Widgets versus Plug-ins: What's the Difference?

A plug-in is a self-contained add-on for WordPress that adds extra functionality to a site. Plug-ins typically include a configuration screen in the Settings or Appearance area (the location depends on the specific plug-in). A widget is a plug-in that adds a drag-and-drop object to the Appearance > Widgets section of a WordPress site. Plug-ins don't always include widgets, but a widget is always generated by a plug-in.

What are widgets?

Widgets—sometimes called *sidebar widgets* because they are often displayed in the sidebar(s) on your site—are little blocks of self-contained code that you can use to display a wide variety of content on your site. Widgets are essentially specialized plug-ins with a unique WYSIWYG interface. WordPress comes with several widgets by default (see the sidebar "Widgets Included with WordPress"), and you can add other widgets by installing them through the Plugins screen. Widgets work by providing a content block that can be added to areas of your site (usually the sidebar, though header and footer widgets are becoming more common) that have been predefined by your theme. Widgets are managed using a drag-and-drop interface in the admin area.

What are plug-ins?

Plug-ins are add-on programs that can modify almost any aspect of your site. Some change the way your site functions, whereas others can do anything from adding content from various sources to turning your WordPress site into an e-commerce shopping cart. Plug-ins may act completely behind the scenes, affecting the operation of your site rather than adding a simple block of content to it.

You manage plug-ins in the Plugin area of the admin area, and most installed plug-ins will add a link to a new configuration screen to a section of the admin sidebar.

> **TIP** The official WordPress Plugin Directory is a great place to find plug-ins and widgets and to read feedback about how well they work. You can find the directory at http://wordpress.org/plugins.

A Click Add New in the Plugins menu to add a new plug-in.

Adding and Activating Plug-ins

Plug-ins enable you to add functionality and features not normally included with WordPress, such as enhanced search engine optimization or integration with third-party services, including Flickr.com. Each plug-in offers something different, which makes it easy to customize your site.

To add plug-ins to your site:

1. In the sidebar menu, choose Plugins > Add New **A**.

   The Install Plugins screen opens **B**.

2. Perform a search to find the plug-in you wish to add. You can search by term, author, or tag. Enter your search term in the text field, and click Search Plugins **C**.

continues on next page

Install Plugins

Screen Options ▾   Help ▾

Search | Upload | Featured | Popular | Newest | Favorites

Plugins extend and expand the functionality of WordPress. You may automatically install plugins from the WordPress Plugin Directory or upload a plugin in .zip format via this page.

Search

[   ] [Search Plugins]

Popular tags

You may also browse based on the most popular tags in the Plugin Directory:

admin AJAX buddypress category comments content email Facebook feed gallery google image images javascript jquery link links login media page pages photo photos plugin Post posts rss seo Share shortcode sidebar social spam stats twitter video widget widgets wordpress youtube

B From the Install Plugins page you can use the links to browse plug-ins available for download or search for specific choices.

Search

[all in one seo   ] [Search Plugins]

C Search for the plug-in you want to add to your site.

Alternately, you can download a plug-in from a non-WordPress source and upload the ZIP file to install the plug-in on your site. To do this, choose Upload instead of Search in the list of options on the Install Plugins screen. After your plug-in uploads, skip to step 4 to activate it.

3. In the list of search results, find the plug-in you wish to add, and click Install Now to begin the installation process ❶. A window appears asking if you are sure you want to install the plug-in. Click OK to continue.

4. When you see the message *Successfully installed the plugin*, click the Activate Plugin link to enable it on your site ❷.

   Once the plug-in has been activated, you will see it in your list of active plug-ins.

Name	Version	Rating	Description
WooCommerce - All In One SEO Pack Details I Install Now	1.3.2	☆☆☆☆☆	This Plugin extends the All in One SEO Pack Plugin (by Michael Torbert) to display the All in One SEO Pack dialog on the Add/Edit Products screen within WooCommerce. Without this Plugin you cannot add/edit/manage All in One SEO Pack meta details which is why I developed this solution. Some features: Title Description Keywords Title Attributes Menu Title Disable Product For more information v… By Visser Labs.
Missing Data All In One SEO Pack Plugin, Add-on Details I Install Now		☆☆☆☆☆	description
All In One SEO Pack Details I Install Now	2.0.2	☆☆☆☆☆	Optimizes your Wordpress blog for Search Engines (Search Engine Optimization). Upgrade to Pro Version Support I Change Log I FAQI Translations Some features: Google Analytics support Support for Custom Post Types Advanced Canonical URLs Fine tune Page Navigational Links Built-in API so other plugins/themes can access and extend functionality ONLY plugin to provide SEO Integrat… By Michael Torbert.

❶ Review the search results, and click Install Now to begin installing your choice.

🔌 Installing Plugin: All in One SEO Pack 2.0.2

Downloading install package from http://downloads.wordpress.org/plugin/all-in-one-seo-pack.zip…

Unpacking the package…

Installing the plugin…

Successfully installed the plugin **All In One SEO Pack 2.0.2**.

Activate Plugin I Return to Plugin Installer

❷ Once your plug-in has downloaded, click Activate Plugin to add it to your site.

5. The main description for the new plug-in contains links to additional configuration areas **❺**. (You can find these in the sidebar under Settings, as well.) Click the Options Configuration Panel link to configure the plug-in.

6. Choose the configuration settings for this plug-in **⑥**, and click Save.

The new plug-in now will use the options you selected to add enhanced functionality to your site's posts and pages.

continues on next page

☐	Plugin	Description
☐	**All In One SEO Pack**	Out-of-the-box SEO for your WordPress blog. Options configuration panel I Upgrade to Pro Version I Donate I Support I Amazon Wishlist
	Deactivate I Edit	
		Version 2.0.2 I By Michael Torbert I Visit plugin site

❺ After your plug-in has been activated, it will appear in your list of active plug-ins. The plug-in we're using for this example displays a handy link to its configuration screen right in its description.

Home Page Settings   ▾

(?)   **Home Title:**

WordPress Visual QuickStart Guide

(?)   **Home Description:**

Learn WordPress the quick and easy way!

(?)   **Home Keywords (comma separated):**

WordPress, blogging, open source, Peachpit, tutorials, walkthroughs

Keyword Settings

(?)   **Use Keywords:**   ◉ Enabled   ○ Disabled

(?)   **Use Categories for META keywords:**   ☐

(?)   **Use Tags for META keywords:**   ☑

(?)   **Dynamically Generate Keywords for Posts Page:**   ☑

⑥ Configure the plug-in to your liking.

TIP Some plug-ins (like the All In One SEO plug-in used in the above example) add additional options to your Edit Post and Edit Page screens ⓗ. Wondering what configuration options are available with which plug-in? Refer to a plug-in's documentation to learn all about it.

All in One SEO Pack

Upgrade to All in One SEO Pack Pro Version

(?)   **Preview Snippet**

http://demo.wpvisualquickstart.com/?p=39

(?)   **Title**

[   ]
[0] characters. Most search engines use a maximum of 60 chars for the title.

(?)   **Description**

[   ]
[0] characters. Most search engines use a maximum of 160 chars for the description.

(?)   **Keywords (comma separated)**

[   ]

(?)   **Robots Meta NOINDEX**   ☐

(?)   **Robots Meta NOFOLLOW**   ☐

(?)   **Disable on this page/post**   ☐

ⓗ In this example, the plug-in has added an additional content area to posts and pages, which can be used for search engine optimization.

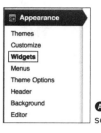

Appearance

Themes
Customize
Widgets
Menus
Theme Options
Header
Background
Editor

Ⓐ The link to the Widgets screen in the Admin sidebar.

Using Widgets

Widgets are designed to be as user-friendly as possible. Once they have been installed, widgets are usable right out of the box and can be managed with a simple drag-and-drop interface.

To use WordPress widgets:

1. In the left sidebar menu, choose Appearance > Widgets to access the Widgets admin screen Ⓐ.

   The Widgets screen opens. On the left side of your screen you see your available widgets. On the right you see all the areas in your theme that will accept widgets Ⓑ.

continues on next page

Available Widgets

Widgets

Screen Options ▾   Help ▾

Available Widgets ▾

Drag widgets from here to a sidebar on the right to activate them. Drag widgets back here to deactivate them and delete their settings.

Archives	**Calendar**
A monthly archive of your site's posts	A calendar of your site's posts
Categories	**Custom Menu**
A list or dropdown of categories	Use this widget to add one of your custom menus as a widget.
Meta	**Pages**
Log in/out, admin, feed and WordPress links	Your site's WordPress Pages
Recent Comments	**Recent Posts**
The most recent comments	The most recent posts on your site
RSS	**Search**
Entries from any RSS or Atom feed	A search form for your site
Tag Cloud	**Text**
Your most used tags in cloud format	Arbitrary text or HTML

Sidebar ▾

Search ▾

Recent Posts ▾

Recent Comments ▾   — *Widgetized Area*

Archives ▾

Categories ▾

Meta ▾

Footer Widget Area One ▾

Footer Widget Area Two ▾

Footer Widget Area Three ▾

Footer Widget Area Four ▾

Inactive Widgets

Inactive Widgets ▾

Drag widgets here to remove them from the sidebar but keep their settings.

Ⓑ The Widgets screen.

2. In the Available Widgets list, locate the widget you want to add to your site **C**.

3. Choose a widget, and drag it to the sidebar where you would like it to appear **D**.

   The widget will expand to show the available configuration options.

4. In the dialog box that opens, choose among any options the widget provides and click Save **E**.

   The content that corresponds with the saved widget will appear on your site. To add additional widgets, simply repeat this process.

TIP You can find an excellent list of available widgets at http://codex.wordpress.org/ WordPress_Widgets.

TIP Widgets are displayed on your site in the order that they are shown in the admin area. You can rearrange them in the Widgets screen by clicking a widget's title and dragging the widget into whatever order you like.

D Dragging a widget into a widgetized sidebar area.

Available Widgets

Drag widgets from here to a sidebar on the right to activate them. Drag widgets back here to deactivate them and delete their settings.

Archives	**Calendar**
A monthly archive of your site's posts	A calendar of your site's posts
Categories	**Custom Menu**
A list or dropdown of categories	Use this widget to add one of your custom menus as a widget.
Meta	**Pages**
Log in/out, admin, feed and WordPress links	Your site's WordPress Pages
Recent Comments	**Recent Posts**
The most recent comments	The most recent posts on your site
RSS	**Search**
Entries from any RSS or Atom feed	A search form for your site
Tag Cloud	**Text**
Your most used tags in cloud format	Arbitrary text or HTML

C Find the widget you want to add to your site.

E Customize the Archives widget by giving it a title and choosing the number of comments you want to display.

Default Widgets

The following widgets are included with a new installation of WordPress:

- Archives: Displays links to the monthly post archive of your blog, either as a list or a drop-down menu.

- Calendar: Shows a calendar with clickable links on dates that feature published posts.

- Categories: Adds either a list or drop-down menu that links to category pages and can display the post counts in each.

- Custom Menu: Easily adds one of your custom menus to your site.

- Meta: Provides links to log in and out, go to the admin area, access RSS feed links, and visit WordPress.org.

- Pages: Displays a menu of your WordPress static pages with the ability to exclude pages and select an ordering method.

- Recent Comments: Displays a list of up to 15 of the most recent comments on your posts.

- Recent Posts: Lists up to 15 of the most recently published posts on your site.

- RSS: Shows entries from any RSS or Atom feed.

- Search: Provides a simple search form for your site.

- Tag Cloud: Displays your most frequently used tags in the popular *cloud* format; tags are listed in a block with commonly used tags displaying in a larger font size than those used infrequently.

- Text: Can be used to include any text or HTML; this widget is highly customizable.

To disable a widget without losing its settings:

1. Select Appearance > Widgets in the left sidebar menu to access the Widgets screen.

2. In the content area on the right side of the screen, locate the widget you wish to disable. Drag it to the Inactive Widgets area below the Available Widgets ❶.

   The widget will no longer be displayed on your site, but the configuration options will be saved. You can re-enable the widget later by simply dragging it from the Inactive Widgets area back into the content area. You may have any number of inactive widgets saved in this way.

Transferring Widgets Between Themes

If you change your theme, your customized widget settings won't be lost: WordPress will automatically transfer your active widgets to the new theme.

If the number of widgetized sidebars is the same in both themes, great! You'll find all your widgets in the same placement and order as they were in your old theme.

If the number of sidebars varies, don't despair. Your widgets will all be located in the first sidebar of the new theme. You can simply drag and drop your widgets into other sidebars and you'll be good to go.

Inactive Widgets

Drag widgets here to remove them from the sidebar but keep their settings.

Recent Comments

❶ The Inactive Widgets area lets you disable a widget without losing any custom settings.

A A number in a bubble next to Plugins lets you know that there are updates waiting for you.

Updating Plug-ins

If a number appears next to Plugins in the sidebar menu, you have plug-ins that can be upgraded **A**.

To upgrade an individual plug-in:

1. Select Plugins from the left sidebar menu. When you see a notice that a new version of your plug-in is available, you can automatically upgrade the plug-in **B**.

2. Click Update Now to continue. The update will automatically install in WordPress.

   The message *Plugin reactivated successfully* signals that your plug-in is up to date and reactivated **C**.

☐ **Jetpack by WordPress.com**
Settings I Deactivate I Edit

Bring the power of the WordPress.com cloud to your self-hosted WordPress. Jetpack enables you to connect your blog to a WordPress.com account to use the powerful features normally only available to WordPress.com users.

Version 2.2.5 I By Automattic I Visit plugin site

There is a new version of Jetpack by WordPress.com available. | View version 2.3 details or update now. |

B If a new version of your plug-in has been released, you will see an update link.

🔌 Update Plugin

Downloading update from http://downloads.wordpress.org/plugin/jetpack.2.3.zip...

Unpacking the update...

Installing the latest version...

Removing the old version of the plugin...

Plugin updated successfully.

| Plugin reactivated successfully. |

C When you see the confirmation message, your plug-in has been successfully updated.

To upgrade plug-ins in bulk:

1. Under the Dashboard link in the left sidebar, click Updates **D**.

   You will see a list of your available plug-in updates. Core WordPress updates are listed here as well.

2. Select the plug-ins you want to update or click the Select All check box to select all of them. Click Update Plugins **E** to continue.

D You can update several plug-ins at once by clicking the Updates link under Dashboard.

Plugins

The following plugins have new versions available. Check the ones you want to update and then click "Update Plugins".

Update Plugins

☑ Select All

☑ **Custom Contact Forms**
You have version 5.1.0.2 installed. Update to 5.1.0.3. View version 5.1.0.3 details.
Compatibility with WordPress 3.5.1: 100% (2 "works" votes out of 2 total)
Compatibility with WordPress 3.5.2: Unknown

☑ **WordPress Importer**
You have version 0.6 installed. Update to 0.6.1. View version 0.6.1 details.
Compatibility with WordPress 3.5.1: 100% (according to its author)
Compatibility with WordPress 3.5.2: Unknown

☑ Select All

Update Plugins

E Select some or all of the plug-ins with available updates to begin the upgrade process.

Your plug-ins will update. You will see a link to each updated plug-in and a message at the bottom letting you know the update was a success **F**.

TIP Always keep your plug-ins up to date. Old or deprecated plug-ins can leave your site vulnerable to hackers and security exploits.

Update Plugins

The update process is starting. This process may take a while on some hosts, so please be patient.

Enabling Maintenance mode...

Updating Plugin Custom Contact Forms (1/2)

Custom Contact Forms updated successfully. Show Details.

Updating Plugin WordPress Importer (2/2)

WordPress Importer updated successfully. Show Details.

Disabling Maintenance mode...

All updates have been completed.

Return to Plugins page | Return to WordPress Updates

F Once you see the message "All updates have been completed," your updating process is done.

Putting It All Together

1. **Install a new plug-in.** How do you find the plug-in you want? Can you install a plug-in from a source other than the Plug-in Directory? How do you activate your new plug-in?

2. **Set up a widget.** Where can you add widgets? How can you modify the widgets you are using? Can you use the same widget twice?

3. **Disable a widget without losing its settings.** Where do you drag a widget to disable it without losing its settings? If you drag the widget back into an active widgetized area, are the settings still there?

4. **Deactivate a plug-in.** Where must you go to deactivate a plug-in? Can you delete an active plug-in without deactivating it first?

Adding Content

The most important part of any Web site is the content. WordPress gives you the ability to easily update your site's content whenever you want, making the process of adding posts and pages simple and painless.

In this chapter, we'll show you the difference between posts and pages; teach you about post formats and how to use them; walk you through the process of adding a new post or editing an existing one; and explain tags, categories, and internal linking. We'll also show you how to post from your desktop, tablet, or smartphone, as well as give you the lowdown on importing your content from another WordPress blog.

Adding Posts

A blog entry or *post* is time-stamped content displayed in reverse chronological order on a Web site. Posts can include HTML formatting, links, images, and media. To help your readers find specific posts, you can organize them into categories and apply searchable tags to posts.

To add a new post:

1. Click Posts in the sidebar menu to access the list of your blog posts **A**. From here you can click Add New to open the Add New Post screen **B**.

Posts	Add New							

All (34) | Published (33) | Draft (1)

Bulk Actions ⬍ Apply   Show all dates ⬍ View all categories ⬍ Filter   ▦ ▤ *34 items* « ‹ 1 of 2 › »

☐	Title	Author	Categories	Tags	💬	Date	SEO Title	SEO Description
☐	**WordPress Site Inspiration - Draft**	Jessica Neuman Beck	WordPress	—	0	2013/06/07 Last Modified	*No title* 🖉	*No description* 🖉
☐	**Tutorial: Using the Theme Customizer**	Jessica Neuman Beck	Tutorials, VQS, WordPress, WordPress 3.+	how-to, theme customizations, tutorial	0	2012/08/24 Published	*No title* 🖉	*No description* 🖉

A Click Posts in the sidebar menu to see all your posts. Click Add New to add a new post.

Add New Post

Enter title here

🖻 Add Media   Visual | Text

B *I* ABC ≡ ≡ " ≡ ≡ ≡ 🔗 ⚡ 🖳 ✂ 🔲 🎬

Path: p

Word count: 0

B The Add New Post screen.

Evolution of WordPress

Permalink: http://www.wpvisualquickstart.com/2013/evolution-of-wordpress/ [Edit]

C The title of your post is used to create the permalink, but you can click Edit to change it.

2. In the Add New Post screen, enter a title for your post. After you do so, you will see a link to the post's URL or *permalink* below the title field **C**. You can change the permalink by clicking the Edit button.

3. Add some content to your post **D**. You can format your content using the formatting toolbar at the top of the visual editor. For more fine-grained control, click the Text tab to edit the markup of your post **E**.

4. To add media or images to your post, click the Add Media button at the top of the editor **F**. (To learn more about managing media, see Chapter 9, "Working with Media.")

continues on next page

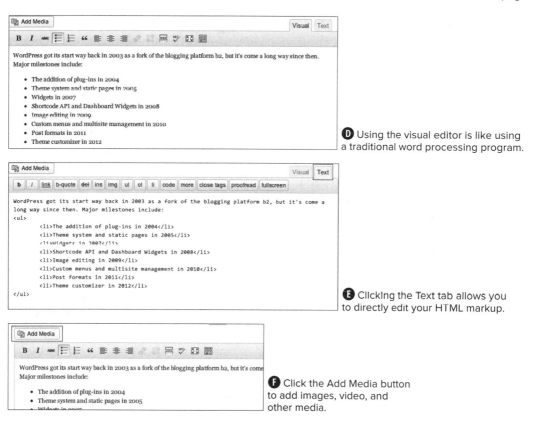

D Using the visual editor is like using a traditional word processing program.

E Clicking the Text tab allows you to directly edit your HTML markup.

F Click the Add Media button to add images, video, and other media.

5. In the right sidebar, add or select a category in the Categories section; add optional information, such as tags, in the Post Tags section **G**. Tags and categories are covered later in this chapter.

6. To see what your post will look like on your site, click Preview in the top of the right sidebar in the Publish section **H**. This will open your post in a new window or tab.

In the Publish section you can also view the post's status and visibility, as well as the publishing schedule **I**. Clicking Edit next to any of these options displays additional publishing options, enabling you to change a post's status to Draft or Pending Review; change the visibility to public (with the option to make the post "sticky," or always visible at the top of the post content section), password protected, or private; or schedule the post for publishing at a later date and time **J**.

Changes you make here will take effect when you publish your post.

7. If everything looks good, close the preview window or tab and return to the Add New Post screen.

8. Click Publish if you are ready to make the post live on your site.

Once your post is published, you will see a "Post published" message at the top of your screen with a link to your new post on your live site **K**.

Categories

All Categories | Most Used

- ☐ Blogging
- ☐ Pictures
- ☐ VQS
- ☑ WordPress
  - ☐ News & Updates
  - ☐ plugins
- ☐ WordPress 3.+
  - ☐ Tutorials

+ Add New Category

Tags

versions, updates | Add

Separate tags with commas

Choose from the most used tags

G Add or select categories and tags for your post. You can choose from a list of tags you've used in the past by clicking the "Choose from the most used tags" link.

Publish

Save Draft | Preview

H Click the Preview button to preview the post on your site before you publish it to the world.

Status: **Draft** Edit

Visibility: **Public** Edit

📅 Publish **immediately** Edit

I Click the Edit link next to each option to customize it.

Status: **Draft**

Draft | ⬍ | OK | Cancel

Visibility: **Public**
- ⦿ Public
  - ☑ Stick this post to the front page
- ◯ Password protected
- ◯ Private

OK | Cancel

📅 Publish **immediately**

07-Jul | ⬍ | 08 , 2013 @ 09 : 09

OK | Cancel

J Choose the publish options for your post and click the OK button next to each one.

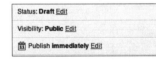

Post published. View post

K Success! You've published a post.

TIP Too many distractions keeping you from concentrating on your post? Toggle the full-screen editor to enter distraction-free writing mode **L**.

The Visual Editor Explained

The visual editor (also known as the WYSIWYG editor) will be familiar to anyone who works with word processing programs. It lets you format your text without touching any code. You can see your changes instantly.

To use the visual editor, simply select the text you'd like to affect and click a formatting button in the toolbar above the body text box. If you're not sure what a button does, hover your cursor over it to see a title (or check out our handy diagram) **M**.

To display additional options for manipulating your content, click the kitchen sink button.

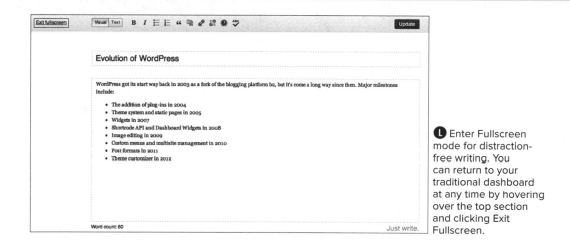

L Enter Fullscreen mode for distraction-free writing. You can return to your traditional dashboard at any time by hovering over the top section and clicking Exit Fullscreen.

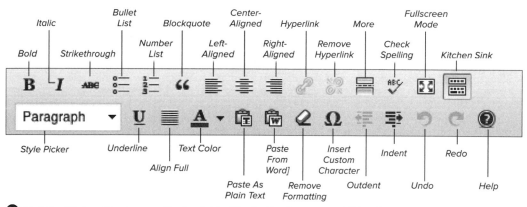

M Click the Kitchen Sink icon on the far right of the toolbar to access additional options such as Underline, Highlight, Insert Custom Character, and Paste From Word.

Using Post Formats

If you're using a theme that supports post formats, you can highlight your content in a different way from standard blog posts. Links, quotes, videos, galleries, and more get special styles (defined by the theme) that will add visual interest to your site.

Using post formats is easy. In the Add Post screen you will see a Format sidebar just below the Publish section. If you're making a standard blog post, just leave it as is. Otherwise, choose from the available formatting options by clicking the appropriate radio button 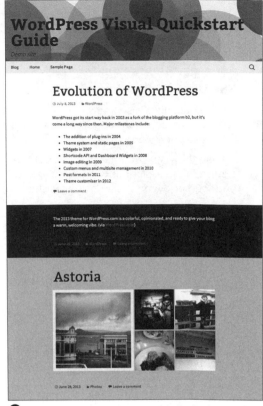. When you save your post, you'll see the special style reflected on your site !

O Posts that use post formats are displayed differently from standard posts.

N Choose a post format to apply special styling to your post.

Adding Pages

Pages are static blocks of content that exist outside the blog chronology. Pages are typically used for content that is updated infrequently, like an About page or a Contact page. When you update a page, the information isn't added to your RSS feed. (To learn more about RSS and syndication, see Chapter 15, "More Ways to Customize WordPress.")

Pages also have the potential to be hierarchical, with top-level parent pages and subpages to organize related blocks of information.

To add a new page:

1. In the sidebar menu, choose Pages > Add New to open the Add New Page screen **A**.

continues on next page

A Click Add New Page to add a new page.

2. Give your page a title. After you type the title, a URL, or permalink, will appear below it. You can edit the permalink by clicking the Edit button **B**.

3. Add some content to your page. You can format your content using the formatting toolbar at the top of the visual editor **C**. For more fine-grained control, click the HTML tab to edit the markup of your page.

4. To add media or images to your page, click one of the icons that appear after the words "Upload/Insert" at the top of the editor. (To learn more about managing media, see Chapter 9, "Working with Media.")

5. Click Publish when you are ready to post the page to your site. You will see "Page published" at the top of the screen **D**.

About Us|

Permalink: http://www.wpvisualquickstart.com/about-us/ [Edit]

B Click the Edit button next to your permalink to change the URL.

C Format new content using the formatting options in the toolbar at the top of the visual editor.

Page published. View page

D Success! Your page has been published.

Ⓔ Select a parent page from the drop-down menu.

Ⓕ A list of your available pages.

About Us
Edit | Quick Edit | Trash | View

Ⓖ Hover over a page title to access the Quick Edit link.

To create subpages:

1. Look in the Page Attributes box on the right of the page editor to see the page hierarchy options. If the page you're creating is an offshoot of or is secondary to another page, you can choose to make it a subpage.

2. You will need an existing page to function as the parent page. Select a page to be the parent in the drop-down menu **Ⓔ**. Click Update Page to save your changes.

To assign a parent from the page list:

1. Click Pages in the sidebar menu to display the list of pages **Ⓕ**.

2. Hover over the page you wish to modify, and click Quick Edit to open the Quick Edit menu **Ⓖ**.

3. Select a parent from the Parent drop-down menu **Ⓗ**.

4. Click Update to save your change. Your page will now display as a subpage of the assigned parent page in the Pages list.

Ⓗ Select a parent page from the drop-down list to assign a hierarchy.

Editing Posts and Pages

The editing process for posts and pages is virtually identical. You can make changes to the title, permalink, and body of the post or page by clicking its title on the listing screen.

To edit an existing post or page:

1. Click the title of your post or page to open the Edit screen **A**.

2. Make the changes the same way you would when creating a new post or page. To change the title, for example, modify the words in the Title field. To add formatting to your body text, use the buttons in the toolbar of the visual editor or add the appropriate HTML tags in the HTML editor **B**.

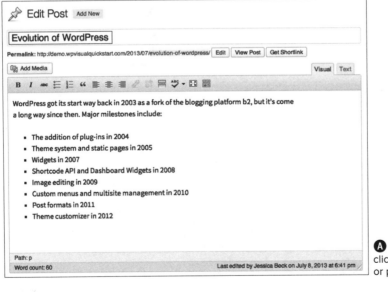

A Open the Edit screen by clicking the title of your post or page.

B Use the formatting buttons to make formatting changes to your post or page.

3. To see what your changes will look like on your site without making them publicly visible, click Preview.

4. When you're happy with your changes, click Update to publish.

TIP To hide a portion of your content, insert a More tag by clicking the More button **C**. Anything after the More tag will be visible only when visitors to your site click to view the full post. A link will be displayed letting viewers know to click for additional content **D**.

- Post formats in 2011
- Theme customizer in 2012

`More...`

WordPress has always maintained a focus on blogging, but recent updates have included more support for the use of the platform as a fully-fledged software solution for all sorts of

C Anything below the More tag will be hidden behind a link on the main page of your site.

WordPress got its start way back in 2003 as a fork of the blogging platform **b2**, but it's come a long way since then. Major milestones include:

- The addition of plug-ins in 2004
- Theme system and static pages in 2005
- Widgets in 2007
- Shortcode API and Dashboard Widgets in 2008
- Image editing in 2009
- Custom menus and multisite management in 2010
- Post formats in 2011
- Theme customizer in 2012

Continue reading →

D Visitors to your site will click the Continue Reading link to see your full post.

Internal Linking

You can easily add a link to an existing post or page on your site.

Inside the edit screen, select the content you want to turn into a link, and then click the Link icon to open the Insert/Edit Link overlay **E**. Click the triangle next to "Or link to existing content" to open the list of your existing posts and pages. (If you have a lot of content, you can enter a keyword in the Search box to narrow your choices **F**.) Choose the content you want to link to; the URL and title will automatically populate the appropriate fields in the top section of the Insert/Edit Link overlay **G**. Specify whether to open the link in a new window or tab.

Finally, click the Add Link button to add your link!

E The Insert/Edit Link overlay. Click the triangle next to "Or link to existing content" to see a list of your posts and pages.

F Use the Search box to help you find the content you want to use for your link.

G When you select the content for your link, the URL and Title fields are automatically populated.

Revisions

Jessica Neuman Beck, 49 mins ago (8 July, 2013 @ 12:32:20)

Jessica Neuman Beck, 51 mins ago (8 July, 2013 @ 12:30:39)

H Each revision to your page is listed in the Revisions section.

Using revisions to revert to a previous version of a page:

1. Open your page in the Edit screen.

2. Scroll down until you see the Revisions section. You'll see a list of revisions, including the name of the person who made each change **H**. Click a revision to compare it to the current version of the page. The Compare Revisions page opens.

3. Use the Previous and Next buttons to quickly scroll through revisions, or use the arrow toggle to view incremental changes **I**. You will see older content on the left and newer updates on the right, with changes highlighted **J**.

4. When you find the older content you want to revert to, click the Restore This Revision button **K**.

continues on next page

| Previous | | Next |

I Toggle between versions by using the Previous and Next buttons or by dragging the arrows from side to side.

🐾 Compare Revisions of "About"

Help ▼

☐ Compare two revisions

| Previous | | Next |

To: Jessica Neuman Beck, 1071 days ago (2 Aug @ 22:21) [Restore This Revision]

Title

About   About

Content

[caption id="attachment_27" align="alignnone" width="300" caption="Matthew Beck and Jessica Neuman Beck"]<a rel="attachment wp-att-27" href="http://www.wordpress28vqs.com/uncategorized/post-subject-here/attachment/beck_640px_mg_0745/"><img class="size-medium wp-image-27" title="beck_640px_mg_0745" src="http://www.wordpress28vqs.com/wp-content/uploads/2009/07/beck_640px_mg_0745-300x225.jpg" alt="Matthew Beck and Jessica Neuman Beck" width="300" height="225" /></a>[/caption]

Jessica Neuman Beck and Matthew Neuman Beck are a designer and a developer who believe good design should be within everyone's reach. We started <a href="http://www.couldbe

[caption id="attachment_27" align="alignnone" width="300" caption="Matthew Beck and Jessica Neuman Beck"]<a href="http://www.wordpress28vqs.com/wp-content/uploads/2009/07/beck_640px_mg_0745.jpg"><img class="size-medium wp-image-27 " title="beck_640px_mg_0745" src="http://www.wordpress28vqs.com/wp-content/uploads/2009/07/beck_640px_mg_0745-300x225.jpg" alt="Matthew Beck and Jessica Neuman Beck by Campbell Salgado Studio" width="300" height="225" /></a>[/caption]

Jessica Neuman Beck and Matthew Neuman Beck are a designer and a developer who believe good design should be within everyone's reach. We started <a

J Changes between an older version (left) and a newer version (right) are highlighted for easy comparison.

To: Jessica Neuman Beck, 1071 days ago (2 Aug @ 22:21) [Restore This Revision]

K When you find the version you want to revert to, click Restore This Revision.

5. Update your page to display the chosen content on your site.

To use Quick Edit to change post options:

1. Click Posts in the sidebar menu to view all your posts **L**.

2. Hover over a post title to see links for the actions you can take **M**. Click Quick Edit to access the Quick Edit panel **N**.

3. Make the changes you want for your post, such as post title, slug (the URL-friendly name of the post, such as your-post-title), the post date, author, privacy settings, categories tags, comments, and post status.

4. Click Update to save your changes.

	Title	Author	Categories	Tags
☐	Evolution of WordPress - Sticky	Jessica Neuman Beck	WordPress	updates, versions
☐	WordPress Site Inspiration - Draft	Jessica Neuman Beck	WordPress	—
☐	Tutorial: Using the Theme Customizer	Jessica Neuman Beck	Tutorials, VQS, WordPress, WordPress 3.+	how-to, theme customizations, tutorial
☐	Tutorial: Flexible Header Images	Jessica Neuman Beck	Tutorials, VQS, WordPress, WordPress 3.+	custom header, how-to, new features, theme customizations, tutorial, wordpress 3.4

L Click Posts to view all your posts.

☐	Evolution of WordPress - Sticky
	Edit I Quick Edit I Trash I View

M Hover over a post title to see the submenu, and then click the Quick Edit link.

N After modifying the available options, click Update to apply your changes.

Setting Up and Using Categories

Categories allow you to group posts together for organizational purposes. Unlike tags, categories can be hierarchical with top-level, or *parent*, categories encompassing an unlimited number of subcategories.

Categories give you a contextual way to organize and locate relevant posts on your site. Categories can be used by your theme or theme widgets to create powerful navigation options. We'll talk more about theme development in Chapter 11, "Getting Fancy with Themes," and Chapter 12, "Advanced Theme Development."

You can add and manage categories by clicking Posts > Categories in the admin sidebar. You can also add them on the fly as you create posts.

To create and manage categories:

1. Access the Categories screen by clicking Posts > Categories in the admin sidebar **A**.

continues on next page

A Click Categories to access the Categories screen.

2. Create a new category by entering a name in the Name field **B**.

3. WordPress automatically generates a category slug when you click Add Category, but if you want to enter your own unique URL-friendly identifier in the Slug field, do so here.

4. If you want to choose a parent, do so using the Parent drop-down menu. The default setting is None, which means your new category will be a top-level, or *parent*, category. If you choose an existing category using the Parent drop-down menu, however, the new category will be a subcategory, or *child* category, of the selected category parent.

5. Click the Add Category button to add your new category. New categories will appear in the list on the right, organized by hierarchy, with child categories displayed below parent categories with a dash in front of them **C**.

Add New Category

Name

Book News

The name is how it appears on your site.

Slug

book-news

The "slug" is the URL-friendly version of the name. It is usually all lowercase and contains only letters, numbers, and hyphens.

Parent

VQS

Categories, unlike tags, can have a hierarchy. You might have a Jazz category, and under that have children categories for Bebop and Big Band. Totally optional.

Description

News about our WordPress Book

The description is not prominent by default; however, some themes may show it.

Add New Category

B To add a new category, all you really need is a name; everything else is optional.

	VQS		vqs	5
	— Book News	News about our WordPress Book	book-news	0

C Child categories appear below parent categories in this list, preceded by a dash.

D Add a new category by clicking the Add New Category link in the post editor.

E Make your new category a subcategory by choosing a parent category from the drop-down list.

F Your new category will appear in the list.

To create a new category in the post editor:

1. Open the post editor, and click the Add New Category link beneath the list of your current categories **D**.

2. Enter the new category name, and choose a parent (if necessary).

3. Click Add New Category **E**.

   You will see a hierarchical list of categories, with your new category and its parent (if any) automatically selected **F**.

TIP If you want to assign a post to an existing category, just select the corresponding check box and you're done.

Using Tags

WordPress provides a simple and powerful tagging mechanism for blog posts.

Tags function like mini-categories, providing additional ways for people to find your posts. Tags can also summarize content, which helps search engines determine relevancy.

Tags are completely optional. When tagging your posts, try using keywords or phrases from your content. Tags are more specific than categories, so a post about a great idea for a big sale at work might be categorized *business*, for example, but it could be tagged *ideas* and *promotions*.

If you display tags on your site, readers can click tags on one post to see other posts that have been tagged with the same thing—even if they're in different categories. So, to continue our example, if you write a post about a brainstorming session with a friend and tag it *ideas*, readers who click that tag will see a list of posts that include the one in which you had some promotional ideas for your business.

To add tags:

1. The easiest method of creating tags is to do it on the fly as you create posts. To add tags to a post, use the post Tags box in the post editor **A**.

    Enter your new tag, and click Add to add it to your post.

2. Add multiple tags all at once by separating them with commas in the entry box **B**.

3. To choose from tags you've used previously, click the "Choose from the most used tags" link. You will see your most used tags displayed as a tag cloud **C**. Click a tag name to add it to your current post.

A Enter tags in the post Tags box and click Add to append them to your post.

B Separate multiple tags with commas.

C You can choose from your most used tags, which are displayed as a tag cloud.

To manage tags:

1. In the sidebar menu, click Posts > Tags to open the Tags screen **D**.

   You'll see a list of all your tags on the right, with a tag cloud on the left showing you which ones have been used most frequently.

2. Click a tag name (in either the tag cloud or the list) to edit the tag. You will see the Edit Tag screen **E**.

continues on next page

📌 Tags

Popular Tags

best practices blogging body conferences **contest** core upgrade custom background **custom header** custom menus **events** features geek rock giveaway giveaways grammar **how-to** links microblogging music navigation **new features** performance permalinks promotion punctuation site customizations social networking speaking gigs stats the book **theme customizations** tips **tutorial** updates URL video what's new Win wordcamp WordPress **wordpress 3.0** wordpress 3.1 wordpress 3.2 writing youtube

Add New Tag

Name
[   ]
The name is how it appears on your site.

Slug
[   ]
The "slug" is the URL-friendly version of the name. It is usually all lowercase and contains only letters, numbers, and hyphens.

	Name	Description	Slug	Posts
☐	admin screen		admin-screen	1
☐	apps		apps	0
☐	best practices		best-practices	1
☐	blogging		blogging	2
☐	body		body	1
☐	book		book	0
☐	conferences		conferences	1
☐	contest		contest	2

Bulk Actions ⬍ [Apply]   65 items « ‹ 1 of 4 › »

[Search Tags]

D All of your tags will be listed in tag cloud format on the left and list format on the right. You can input a new tag by using the Add New Tag form below the tag cloud.

📌 Edit Tag

Name
[how-to   ]
The name is how it appears on your site.

Slug
[how-to   ]
The "slug" is the URL-friendly version of the name. It is usually all lowercase and contains only letters, numbers, and hyphens.

Description
[   ]
The description is not prominent by default; however, some themes may show it.

[Update]

E Edit tags and tag slugs here.

3. Make the changes to your tag, and click Update.

TIP From the Tags screen you can also remove tags that are no longer relevant to your site or content. Select the tags you want to delete and choose Delete from the Bulk Actions drop-down menu ⑥. You must click Apply to delete the tags.

⑥ Delete tags you no longer need by using Bulk Actions.

Other Ways to Add Content

In addition to posting from your site's admin area, you can also post directly from your browser using the Press This extension, or you can post from your smartphone or tablet using the official WordPress apps. You can even make quick content additions straight from your admin Dashboard using the QuickPress widget.

If you would like to import content from another site, WordPress makes that easy, too. You can import directly from another WordPress blog or from a number of third-party blogging services.

Using QuickPress

The simplest way to create a new post on your WordPress site is to use the QuickPress widget on the Dashboard. From QuickPress you can add a title, content, and tags right from the main screen of your Dashboard, then publish it immediately or save it as a draft. You can even add media, such as images, videos, or music **A**.

Simplest, however, isn't necessarily *best*. QuickPress may be great for quick posts, but because there is no way to select a category, any post you make from here will be assigned to the default. If that works for you, great! Otherwise, you may want to use QuickPress to jot down post ideas rather than using it as a publishing tool. If you save your QuickPress posts as drafts, you can access them later through the Posts screen. There you have full access to all the post-editing features.

A QuickPress is a quick, easy way to add a post or create a draft from your WordPress dashboard.

Posting with the Press This browser extension:

1. Install the Press This browser extension by logging in to your WordPress admin area, choosing Settings > Writing, and dragging the Press This shortcut into your browser's toolbar **B**.

2. Find content on the Web that you'd like to add to your blog, and click the Press This link in your toolbar. The Press This window opens **C**.

Press This

Press This is a bookmarklet: a little app that runs in your browser and lets you grab bits of the web.

Use Press This to clip text, images and videos from any web page. Then edit and add more straight from Press This before you save or publish it in a post on your site.

Drag-and-drop the following link to your bookmarks bar or right click it and add it to your favorites for a posting shortcut.

[Press This]

B Drag the Press This extension to the toolbar of your browser to install it.

C When you find content you want to share, click the Press This link in your browser's toolbar to open the Press This window.

3. Customize your post by adding images and quotes from the original source, as well as your own thoughts and comments 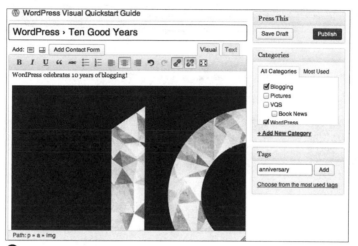.

4. Choose Save Draft to save your post for later, or click Publish to post it directly to your site .

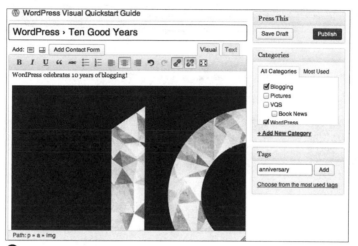

D Customize your post by adding your own text. You can also add images and quotes from the original source.

E Publish or save your post as a draft.

Posting from a smartphone or tablet:

1. Install the WordPress app from your device's app store .

2. Open the WordPress app, and enter your credentials to log in to your WordPress admin .

F Find and install the official WordPress app from your device's app store.

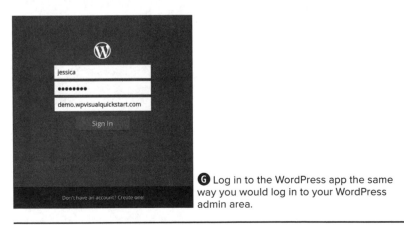

G Log in to the WordPress app the same way you would log in to your WordPress admin area.

H Click the plus sign next to Posts to add a new post.

3. Click the plus sign next to Posts **H** to open the New Post screen **I**.

4. Add images, video, or attachments by using the icons at the lower right **J**.

continues on next page

Cancel	New Post	Publish

Title:

Tags: Separate tags with commas

Categories:

Tap here to begin writing

I Enter a title, tags, category, and body to create a new post.

Add Photo from Library

Take Photo

J Use the icons on the lower right to add media, such as images, video, and attachments.

5. Preview your post by clicking the eye icon on the lower left **K**. Change the Publish settings by clicking the gear icon **L**.

6. Click the Publish button to send your post to your site.

K The eye icon on the lower left will show you a preview of your post.

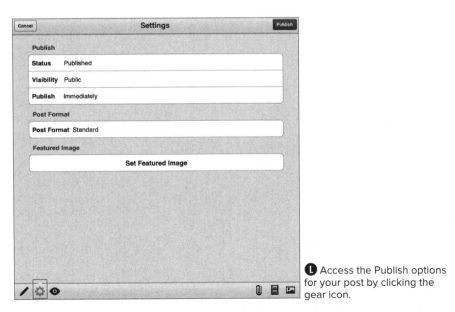

L Access the Publish options for your post by clicking the gear icon.

Importing from another WordPress blog:

1. Log in to the blog *from which* you are exporting, and go to Tools > Export. Choose the options for your export, and click Download Export File **M**.

2. Log in to the site *to which* you are importing, and choose Tools > Import. Find the WordPress Importer in the list **N** and click it, then click Install Now to add the WordPress Importer plug-in **O**.

continues on next page

Ⓣ Export

When you click the button below WordPress will create an XML file for you to save to your computer.

This format, which we call WordPress eXtended RSS or WXR, will contain your posts, pages, comments, custom fields, categories, and tags.

Once you've saved the download file, you can use the Import function in another WordPress installation to import the content from this site.

Choose what to export

⦿ All content

This will contain all of your posts, pages, comments, custom fields, terms, navigation menus and custom posts.

○ Posts
○ Pages
○ Feedback
○ Portfolio

[Download Export File]

M Choose the export options for your source file.

Ⓣ Import

If you have posts or comments in another system, WordPress can import those into this site. To get started, choose a system to import from below:

Blogger	Install the Blogger importer to import posts, comments, and users from a Blogger blog.
Blogroll	Install the blogroll importer to import links in OPML format.
Categories and Tags Converter	Install the category/tag converter to convert existing categories to tags or tags to categories, selectively.
LiveJournal	Install the LiveJournal importer to import posts from LiveJournal using their API.
Movable Type and TypePad	Install the Movable Type importer to import posts and comments from a Movable Type or TypePad blog.
RSS	Install the RSS importer to import posts from an RSS feed.
Tumblr	Install the Tumblr importer to import posts & media from Tumblr using their API.
WordPress	Import posts, pages, comments, custom fields, categories, and tags from a WordPress export file.

If the importer you need is not listed, search the plugin directory to see if an importer is available.

N Click the WordPress importer to begin the installation process.

Install Importer   ✕

Description   Installation   Changelog   FAQ   Other Notes

Description

[Install Now]

The WordPress Importer will import the following content from a WordPress export file:

FYI

Version: 0.6.1

- Posts, pages and other custom post types
- Comments
- Custom fields and post meta
- Categories, tags and terms from custom taxonomies
- Authors

Author: wordpressdotorg
Last Updated: 102 days ago
Requires WordPress Version: 3.0 or higher
Compatible up to: 3.6
Downloaded: 5,072,061 times

For further information and instructions please see the Codex page on Importing Content

WordPress.org Plugin Page »
Plugin Homepage »

Average Rating
★ ★ ★ ☆ ☆
(based on 272 ratings)

O Click Install Now to install the WordPress importer.

---

3. Click Activate Plugin & Run Importer **P**.

4. Select the export file you created in step 1, and click Upload File And Import **Q**.

Installing Plugin: WordPress Importer 0.6.1

Downloading install package from `http://downloads.wordpress.org/plugin/wordpress-importer.0.6.1.zip`...

Unpacking the package...

Installing the plugin...

Successfully installed the plugin **WordPress Importer 0.6.1**.

Activate Plugin & Run Importer | Return to Importers

P Click Activate Plugin & Run Importer to begin the import process.

Import WordPress

Howdy! Upload your WordPress eXtended RSS (WXR) file and we'll import the posts, pages, comments, custom fields, categories, and tags into this site.

Choose a WXR (.xml) file to upload, then click Upload file and import.

Choose a file from your computer: (Maximum size: 5 MB) [Choose File] wordpressvisu...7-08 (1).xml

[Upload file and import]

Q Locate the export file you created, and run the importer.

Importing from Other Blogging Services

WordPress supports importing from many other blogging services, such as Blogger, Movable Type, and Tumblr.

In your admin area, go to Tools > Import to see the available importers. (If you don't see the blogging platform you want to import from on the list, you may need to search the WordPress Plugin Directory to find the appropriate importer.) After you locate your importer, follow the instructions to install it and add your content to WordPress.

5. Choose whether to assign posts to existing users or to create new users, and choose whether to download and import file attachments. Click Submit to begin the import process ⓡ.

6. When your import is complete, you will see a success message ⓢ. Your posts, pages, and media files are now imported.

🔧 Import WordPress

Assign Authors

To make it easier for you to edit and save the imported content, you may want to reassign the author of the imported item to an existing user of this site. For example, you may want to import all the entries as `admin`s entries.

If a new user is created by WordPress, a new password will be randomly generated and the new user's role will be set as subscriber. Manually changing the new user's details will be necessary.

1. Import author: **Matt Beck (matt)**
   or create new user with login name: _____
   or assign posts to an existing user: [Matt Beck ⬍]
2. Import author: **Jessica Neuman Beck (jessica)**
   or create new user with login name: _____
   or assign posts to an existing user: [Jessica Beck ⬍]

Import Attachments

☑ Download and import file attachments

[Submit]

ⓡ Assign your posts to existing authors or create new ones, and choose whether to download and import media files.

🔧 Import WordPress

All done. Have fun!

Remember to update the passwords and roles of imported users.

ⓢ Your import is complete.

Putting It All Together

1. **Create a test post.** Using QuickPress, create a post and set the title to "My Test Post." Can you create a category to place it in at the same time? Try adding tags to the post. When you are finished, publish it to your site. How and where on your site is the post displayed?

2. **Edit your test post.** Can you add an image gallery to your post? What categories are assigned to it?

3. **Create a new page.** Try using the same title as your test post, "My Test Post." Will this cause any problems? Where will the page be displayed on your site?

4. **Create a link to your test post.** Edit your new page to add an internal link to your test post.

Menus

When you set up a new WordPress site, your theme's navigation menu automatically lists all your pages in alphabetical order. But what if you want to list only your main pages in the navigation? What if you want custom menu items or more than one menu?

Custom menus to the rescue! WordPress custom menus make it easy to add, change, and move menus and menu items with a slick drag-and-drop interface.

In this chapter, we'll show you how to create custom menus. We'll show you how to add your menus to preassigned menu areas in your theme and how to add a menu as a sidebar widget. We'll also show you how to edit and update your menus to keep everything on your site up to date.

In This Chapter

Setting Up Menus

Before you can take advantage of all the things custom menus have to offer, you'll need to set up your first menu. Fortunately, that's easy to do.

To customize your default menu:

1. In the admin area, go to Appearance > Menus to open the Edit Menus page.

   By default, your first menu has the name Menu 1 and shows all the pages on your site, with a custom link to your site's home page in the first position **A**.

A Click Appearance in the sidebar menu to expand the Appearance submenu. Click Menus to manage the menus.

Menu Name | Main Navigation

B Change the menu's name to something descriptive.

Home | Custom ▾

URL
http://demo.wpvisualquickstart.com/

Navigation Label | Title Attribute
Home |

Move _Down one_

Remove | Cancel

C Expand the menu item to edit it.

Move _Down one_

D Click to move the menu item down the list.

Blog | Page ▾

About Us | Page ▾

Our Work | Page ▾

E You can drag a menu item to a new position.

Remove | Cancel

F Click Remove to delete the menu item.

Reference | Page ▾

Theme Building | Page ▾

WordPress Templates | Page ▾

G Drag a menu item into an indented position to create a submenu.

Reference | Page ▾

Theme Building _sub item_ | Page ▾

WordPress Templates | Page ▾

H Theme Building is now a submenu of Reference.

2. Change the name of your menu to something that will help you identify it and locate it later **B**.

3. Click the triangle to the right of your first menu item to expand its options **C**. With these, you can modify the title and add a title attribute (the alternative text that appears when a cursor hovers over the menu item). You can also change the position of the menu item: Either click the links in the Move section **D**, or drag and drop the menu item into a new position **E**.

   To delete the menu item entirely, click Remove **F**.

4. Repeat step 3 with all the default menu items.

5. To create a submenu, drag one menu item under another until it shows an indent **G**. When you let go of that menu item, it will display the words "sub item" next to its title **H**.

6. When you are happy with your menu, click Create Menu.

   Your menu will be saved and will display a new section called Menu Settings below it **I**. From this section, you can specify whether new top-level (parent) pages appear in your menu automatically, as well as choose to add your menu to a predefined area in your theme (more on that in the next section of this chapter).

Menu Settings

Auto add pages | ☐ Automatically add new top-level pages to this menu
Theme locations | ☐ Navigation Menu

I The Menu Settings area contains optional settings for your menu.

To create a new menu:

1. In your WordPress admin area, go to Appearance > Menus. Click the "create a new menu" link **J**.

2. Give your menu a name, and click Create Menu **K**.

3. Add menu items using the options on the left. You can choose from the pages on your site **L**, a custom link to any URL **M**, or any of your categories **N**. When you have made a selection, click Add To Menu to add it to your menu.

4. Click Save Menu.

TIP Click the Screen Options tab **O** to expose more options from which you can choose menu items, including Posts, Links, Categories, Tags, Format, and Pages. Click the check box next to any of these options to select or deselect them for display.

Edit your menu below, or create a new menu.

J Click this link to create a new menu.

Menu Name	Secondary Menu		Create Menu

Give your menu a name above, then click Create Menu.

K Enter a name for your menu, and click Create Menu.

Pages

Most Recent | View All | Search

- ☐ About Us
- ☐ Blog
- ☑ Home
- ☐ Sample Page
- ☐ Our Work
- ☐ Reference
  - ☐ Our Theme
  - ☐ Example Plugin
  - ☐ Theme Building
  - ☐ WordPress Templates

Select All | Add to Menu

L Check the boxes next to pages you wish to add to your menu.

Links

URL | http://twitter.com/askWP\

Link Text | Twitter

Add to Menu

M Enter a full URL and title to add any link to your menu.

Categories

Most Used | View All | Search

- ☐ WordPress
  - ☐ News & Updates
  - ☐ plugins
- ☑ WordPress 3.+
  - ☐ Tutorials
- ☐ Uncategorized
- ☐ VQS
- ☐ Photos
- ☐ Blogging
- ☐ Pictures

Select All | Add to Menu

N Check the boxes next to categories you wish to add to your menu.

Show on screen

☐ Posts ☑ Links ☑ Categories ☐ Tags ☐ Format ☑ Pages

Show advanced menu properties

☐ Link Target ☐ CSS Classes ☐ Link Relationship (XFN) ☐ Description

Screen Options ▲

Edit Menus | Manage Locations

O Advanced menu properties enable you to control the behavior of links in your menu.

Menu Settings

Auto add pages   ☐ Automatically add new top-level pages to this menu

Theme locations   ☑ Navigation Menu

Ⓐ Check the name of the location from your theme where you would like the menu to display.

▣ Edit Menus | Manage Locations

Your theme supports 1 menu. Select which menu you would like to use below.

Theme Location	Assigned Menu
Navigation Menu	Main Navigation ⬍ Edit │ Use new menu

Save Changes

Ⓑ Select the name of the location from your theme where you would like the menu to display.

Main Widget Area   ▼

Appears in the footer section of the site.

Search   ▼

Custom Menu

Ⓒ Drag the custom menu widget into the desired location.

Custom Menu   ▼

Title:
More Links

Select Men   Main Navigation
             ✓ Secondary Menu

Delete I Close   Save

Ⓓ Select the menu you wish the widget to display.

Adding Menus to Your Site

Once you create a menu, you can add it to your site in a couple of different ways. If your theme natively supports custom menus, you can quickly and easily specify which menu goes where. If your theme doesn't support custom menus (or if you'd like to display an alternate menu in a different spot), you can add your custom menu as a widget.

Using theme menu areas:

1. Go to Appearance > Menus, and scroll down to the bottom of your menu. Under Menu Settings, find the section called Theme Locations.

2. Use the check box to assign your menu to the supported location in the theme **Ⓐ**.

   Alternately, you can click the Manage Locations tab at the top of the Menus screen. The supported theme locations will display. Select the menu you want to use from the drop-down **Ⓑ**.

3. Click Save Changes to update the menu to your site.

Adding menus as widgets:

1. Go to Appearance > Widgets. Find the Custom Menu widget, and drag it into a widgetized area **Ⓒ**.

2. In the Title field, enter a title for your menu. This will display above your menu on your site.

3. Choose the custom menu you want to display in your widget **Ⓓ**.

4. Click Save to save your custom menu widget.

Editing Menus

Making changes or updates to your custom menus is simple and painless. In addition to adjusting the settings we've already discussed, you can make each menu item open in a new window or tab, use special CSS classes, take advantage of link relationships, or include a description.

To edit a menu:

1. Go to Appearance > Menus. At the top of the screen, choose the menu you want to edit from the drop-down and click Select **A**.

2. To change the order of your menu items, drag and drop them into the desired position. You can also click the Move links to change the placement of your menu item **B**.

3. Click the triangle to the right of the menu item's title to expand its options. By default, you can edit the title or the title attributes (alternative text that appears when a cursor hovers over the menu item). If your menu item is a custom link, you can also edit the URL.

A Click Select to edit the selected menu.

B Drag into position, or click to change the order of the menu items.

4. Click the Screen Options tab at the top of the screen to see all the possible options for your menu item **C**. Toggle the check boxes next to the options you'd like to enable, and the appropriate fields will appear in the options for each menu item **D**.

5. Delete items from your menu by clicking the Remove link at the bottom of the item **E**.

6. When you're happy with your menu, click the Save Menu button.

C Check the additional options you wish to see.

E Click Remove to delete menu items.

D Add additional behavior and information to your menu links.

Putting It All Together

1. **Create a new menu.** Add a link to a page on your site as well as a custom link to an off-site URL. How do those display in your menu?

2. **Reorder your menu items.** Can you move menu items by dragging and dropping them? What other method can you use to change the order of your menu items?

3. **Assign a menu to a theme location.** Where in the Edit Menu screen can you do this? Are there other ways to assign a menu to a theme location?

4. **Enable additional options for your menu items.** How do you specify that a link opens in a new window or tab?

Working with Media

Video, audio, images . . . how do you manage them all? With the Media Library tools included with WordPress, keeping track of all of these components is a breeze. The Media Library lets you upload and display audio files, videos, and images.

In this chapter, we'll show you how to upload and manage your media. We'll walk you through the process of creating an image gallery to showcase related images, and we'll talk a little about the pros and cons of using a third-party service like YouTube to host your video content.

In This Chapter

Using the Media Library

The WordPress Media Library is the section of your WordPress admin screen where you can manage your media uploads Ⓐ. Here, you can edit, view, and delete media files. You can select multiple files for bulk deletion, and you can use the Search feature to quickly locate particular uploads.

You can filter the list to show only images, audio, video, or unattached files by clicking the corresponding links at the top of the list. Next to each of these filters is a number showing how many of that type of file you have in your library Ⓑ.

Media is arranged by date, with the most recently uploaded files appearing first in the list. An icon at the left of the filename shows you the type of file (a thumbnail for images or a static icon for many other common types of files), and at the right you can see the name of the user who uploaded the file, the post or page it is attached to (if any), the number of comments, and the date the file was uploaded Ⓒ.

Ⓐ An overview of the Media Library.

All (52) | Images (47) | Audio (2) | Video (2) | Unattached (6)

Ⓑ Filter results by using the links at the top of the overview screen.

Ⓒ Each file in the Media Library shows you information about the file type and its related post or page.

Media Library   Add New

D To upload an image to the Media Library, begin by clicking the Add New link.

To upload an image through the Media Library:

1. Click the Add New button at the top of the Media Library screen **D**, or choose Media > Add New in the left sidebar menu.

2. On the Upload New Media page, click Select Files **E** to open the file selection dialog box.

3. Select the images you wish to upload, and then click Choose. Your uploads will appear below the file selection area, each with a progress bar that shows the status of the file **F**.

4. When your files finish uploading, notice that each file's progress bar is replaced by an edit link **G**.

Upload New Media

Drop files here
or
Select Files

You are using the multi-file uploader. Problems? Try the browser uploader instead.

Maximum upload file size: 5MB.

E Choose the file or files you want to upload.

| 2012-09-19 10.00.38.jpg | 100% |
| 2012-08-30 14.15.10.jpg | 0% |

F A progress bar shows you the completion percentage of each upload.

| | 2012-09-19 10.00.38 | Edit |
| | 2012-08-30 14.15.10 | Edit |

G When an image finishes uploading, you will see an Edit link next to it.

TIP Want an even easier way to upload files? Simply drag the files you want into the file selection area **H**.

To add an image from a page or a post:

1. Click the Add Media button at the top of the editing screen to open the Insert Media window **I**.

21 PM	119 KB	JPEG image
1:40 AM	407 KB	JPEG image
5:34 PM	282 KB	JPEG image
29 AM	243 KB	JPEG image
47 AM	233 KB	JPEG image
0 PM	387 KB	JPEG image
1 PM	196 KB	JPEG image
1 PM	1.1 MB	JPEG image
1:41 AM	1.8 MB	JPEG image
0:59 AM	542 KB	JPEG image
2:21 PM	632 KB	JPEG image
09 PM	180 KB	JPEG image
7 PM	176 KB	JPEG image
9 PM	1.5 MB	JPEG image
0 PM	349 KB	JPEG image

Upload New Media

Drop files here
or
2011-02-15 11.40.31.jpg   Select Files

H You also can drag and drop a file directly into the uploader to start uploading.

Add Media

📌 Add New Post

Working from the Coffee Shop

Permalink: http://www.wpvisualquickstart.com/2013/wor

🖼 Add Media   🗐 Add Contact Form

B *I* ᴬᴮᶜ ☰ ☰ 66 ☰ ☰ ☰ ✐

A great thing about WordPress: you can use it anyw

I Click Add Media to add an image to a post or page.

2. Click Select Files to upload a new image (or drag the image into the file selection area) **J**. If your image is already in the Media Library, click the Media Library tab to find and select it **K**.

continues on next page

Insert Media	Insert Media ✕
Create Gallery	Upload Files Media Library
Set Featured Image	
Insert from URL	

Drop files anywhere to upload

Select Files

☐ Scale images to match the large size selected in <u>image options</u> (800 × 1024).

Maximum upload file size: 5MB.

Insert into post

J Upload a file by clicking the Select Files button.

K Choose an already uploaded file from the Media Library.

3. After you choose your image, a check mark appears next to your selection. Notice the new Attachment Details section on the right, as well. Here, you can quickly add or edit the image title, caption, alt text, and description **L**. At the bottom of this section you can also choose display settings, such as image alignment and size **M**.

4. Click Insert Into Post (below the Attachment Details section) to add the image to your post or page.

5. Finish your post or page as you usually would (you can find more information about posts and pages in Chapter 7, "Adding Content"), and click the Publish button.

   Your uploaded image will appear along with your post or page.

TIP You can also insert an image from an external URL. Click the Insert From URL link in the Insert Media window sidebar, and enter the URL of the image you'd like to use **N**.

check mark   Attachment Details

L When you select a file to add to your post, it is marked with a check mark. You can edit the image's information in the Attachment Details section.

M At the bottom of the Attachment Details section you can choose display settings.

N Click Insert From URL to add an image using a URL.

Media Library Add New

All (46) | Images (41) | Audio (2) | Video (2) | Unattached (3)

| Bulk Actions | ↕ | Apply | Show all dates | ↕ | Filter |

	File
☐	
☐	2012-08-30 14.15.10 JPG
☐	2012-09-19 10.00.38 JPG

A Click the title of the image you want to edit.

Editing Images

Sometimes you need to make changes to your images on the fly. When you do, you can crop, resize, flip, and scale images directly from the Media Library.

To edit an image:

1. If you're not already in the Media Library, open it by clicking Media in the left sidebar menu. You will see a list of media files. Click the thumbnail image or title of the image you wish to edit **A**.

2. In the Edit Media screen, edit or add to the title, caption, and description fields **B**. If these are the only changes you need to make, click Update to save your changes. Otherwise, continue to step 3 (your changes will carry over to the next screen).

continues on next page

Edit Image ———

B Edit the title, caption, and description. To access more editing options, click the Edit Image button below the image preview.

3. To edit the image itself, click the Edit Image button to open the built-in image editor included in WordPress **C**.

4. If you wish to change the size of the image, click Scale Image on the right **D**.

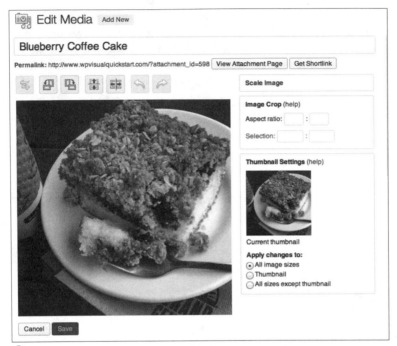

C Use the built-in image editor to make changes to your image.

Scale Image

You can proportionally scale the original image. For best results the scaling should be done before performing any other operations on it like crop, rotate, etc. Note that if you make the image larger it may become fuzzy.

Original dimensions 1280×1280

1280 × 1280 [Scale]

D Scale your image by entering your desired dimensions in the height and width boxes.

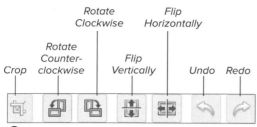

Crop | Rotate Counter-clockwise | Rotate Clockwise | Flip Vertically | Flip Horizontally | Undo | Redo

E Use the icons at the top of the image preview to edit your image.

5. Use the icons above the image to crop, rotate, or flip your image **E**. To crop the image, simply click and drag on the image to set the area you wish to crop, and then click the Crop button **F**.

6. Under Thumbnail Settings on the right, select whether to have your changes apply to all versions of this image, the thumbnail only, or everything except the thumbnail **G**.

7. If you haven't already made additions or changes to the Title, Caption, or Description fields, you can do so here in the Edit Media screen.

8. Click Update to save your image edits **H**.

F Select an area of the image to activate the Crop button; click it to crop the image.

Thumbnail Settings (help)

Current thumbnail

Apply changes to:
- All image sizes
- Thumbnail
- All sizes except thumbnail

G Choose whether to apply your changes to all image sizes, just the thumbnail, or everything except the thumbnail.

Save

Uploaded on: Jul 19, 2013 @ 9:27

File URL:
http://www.wpvisualquickstart.com/wp-content

File name: 2012-09-19-10.00.38.jpg

File type: JPG

Dimensions: 1280 x 1280

Delete Permanently | Update

H Click Update to save your changes.

Creating and Managing Image Galleries

Galleries are a great way to organize and share groups of images.

To create a gallery:

1. Create the post or page where you want to add the photo gallery.

2. Click the Add Media icon at the top of the edit screen to launch the Insert Media window. Click the Create Gallery link on the left **A**.

A Click Create Gallery to begin the gallery creation process.

3. Upload the files you want to add to your gallery, or select them from the Media Library (see instructions in previous section). Your selected images will appear with a check box in the upper-right corner **B**.

When you have selected all the images you want to include in your gallery, click the "Create a new gallery" button.

4. In the Edit Gallery screen, you can drag and drop your images to reorder them. You can also choose your Gallery Settings in the right sidebar **C**. Choose whether clicking an image will open the image's attachment page or the image itself, the number of columns your gallery will have, whether the images will display in a random order, and whether the gallery will show as a thumbnail grid or a slideshow.

continues on next page

Create
A New Gallery

B Click "Create A New Gallery" to convert your chosen images into a gallery.

C Drag and drop to reorder your images; choose gallery options on the right.

5. Click the Insert Gallery button to add the gallery to your post or page ⓓ. To make additional changes to your gallery, click the photo placeholder icon, and then click the Edit Gallery button ⓔ.

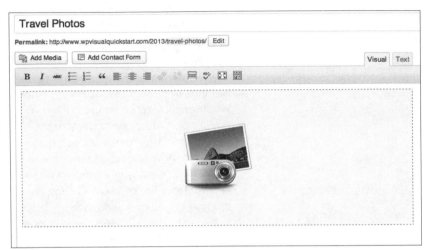

ⓓ The gallery placeholder in the Edit Post screen.

ⓔ Click the Edit Gallery button to make additional changes to the gallery.

6. Click the Publish button on the far right to publish the gallery page or post to your site **F**.

F A thumbnail grid gallery in a published post.

Using Audio and Video Files

Audio and video files can add a new layer of interaction to your site. You can share a lecture, a screencast, or your child's first piano recital as easily as sharing photos.

WordPress natively supports both audio and video files. That's right, you no longer have to use third-party services or plug-ins to host songs, videos, or audio snippets on your site. (If you *do* want to use a third-party service, however, the embedding process is easy.)

To upload an audio file:

1. Follow the steps under "To upload an image through the Media Library," but select your audio file in the File Upload dialog box. When your audio file has uploaded, you will see an Edit link next to it **A**.

2. Click the Edit link to preview the file, as well as add a caption and a description **B**.

🎵	myvoice	Edit

A Click the Edit link to access more details about your audio file.

🖼️ **Edit Media** Add New

myvoice

Permalink: http://www.wpvisualquickstart.com/?attachment_id=608 View Attachment Page Get Shortlink

▶ 00:00   00:00 🔊 ▬▬

Caption

Description

b *i* link b-quote del ins img ul ol li code close tags

"Audio file".

Save

📅 Uploaded on: **Jul 19, 2013 @ 12:21**

File URL:
http://www.wpvisualquickstart.com/wp-content

File name: **myvoice.m4a**

File type: **M4A**

Mime-type: **audio/mp4**

Length: **0:09**

Bitrate: **199.210253906kb/s**

Delete Permanently   Update

B Preview or modify details about your audio file.

C The icon used to represent audio files in the Media Library.

ATTACHMENT DETAILS

> myvoice.m4a
> July 19, 2013
> Delete Permanently

Title	myvoice
Caption	Demonstrating WordPress' built-in audio player.
Description	"Audio file".

ATTACHMENT DISPLAY SETTINGS

Link To	Media File

Insert into post

D Attachment details for an audio file.

Follow the sound of my voice

▶ 00:00   00:00 🔊 ▬▬▬

Demonstrating WordPress' built-in audio player. Click above to listen!

E A published post containing an audio file.

---

3. Click the Update button. Your uploaded audio file will appear in the Media Library with a musical note icon **C**.

To add an audio file to a post or page:

1. Find the Upload Media button at the top of the editing screen; click it to open the Insert Media window.

2. Click Select Files to upload a new audio file (or drag the file into the file selection area). If your audio file is already in the Media Library, click the Media Library tab to find and select it.

3. After you choose your file, notice the check mark next to your selection. In the Attachment Details section on the right, you can quickly add or edit the title, caption, alt text, and description of your audio file **D**.

4. Click Insert Into Post to add the audio file to your post or page.

5. Finish your post or page as you usually would (you can find more information about posts and pages in Chapter 7, "Adding Content"), and click the Publish button.

   Your uploaded audio file will appear along with your post or page **E**.

Third-Party Video Hosting

Video content can enhance your site, but at a price. For example, it can consume vast amounts of space on your site, as well as put you at risk of exceeding your hosting bandwidth if your video gets a lot of views. Third-party video hosting can be a great way to share video content without sacrificing too much server space.

Benefits of using a third-party solution include the following:

- Many services (like YouTube, Vimeo, and Viddler) are free for personal use; YouTube also allows commercial content.
- Added sharing features make it easy to cross-post your content elsewhere.
- More ways to find your video content means more potential views.
- Your video can be viewed at many different sizes and resolutions, allowing for the best viewing experience.

Using a third-party solution has a few drawbacks as well:

- Many services (like Vimeo and Viddler) do not allow commercial content on their free accounts.
- You are subject to the terms and conditions of the third-party service, which can limit your upload options.
- If the service crashes, your video will be unavailable. Always keep a backup!

To add a video to a post or a page:

1. Find the Upload Media button at the top of the editing screen, and click it to open the Insert Media window.

2. Click Select Files to upload a new video file (or drag the file into the file selection area). If your video file is already in the Media Library, click the Media Library tab to find and select it. After you do, you will see a check mark next to your selection.

3. If you want to add or edit the title, caption, alt text, or description of your video file, use the Attachment Details section now (on the right) **F**.

4. Click Insert Into Post to add the video file to your post or page.

5. Finish your post or page as you usually would (you can find more information about posts and pages in Chapter 7, "Adding Content"), and click the Publish button.

Your uploaded video will appear along with your post or page **G**.

F Select the video file you want to add, and click the "Insert Into Post" button.

G A published post containing a video.

To add a video to a post or a page using an embed code:

1. Locate the embed code for the video you wish to add to your post or page. In our example, the embed code is found by clicking the Share This Video link and choosing the Embed Code option **H**. The location of this code varies depending on the video hosting site; our example is from Vimeo.com.

2. Select the embed code provided by the site, and copy it to your clipboard (Ctrl+C in Windows, Command+C on a Mac).

H Find the embed code for the video you want to embed, and copy it to your clipboard.

3. Open the post editor, and click the Text tab to access the raw markup for your post.

4. Paste the embed code into the body of your post **I**, and click Save.

5. Open your post in the browser to view your embedded video **J**.

| Add Media | | | | | | | | | | | | Visual | **Text** |

b | i | link | b-quote | del | ins | img | ul | ol | li | code | more | close tags | fullscreen

```
<iframe src="http://player.vimeo.com/video/38469668" width="500" height="375" frameborder="0"
webkitAllowFullScreen mozallowfullscreen allowFullScreen></iframe> <p><a
href="http://vimeo.com/38469668">Quick Grammar</a> on <a href="https://vimeo.com">Vimeo</a>.</p>
```

I Click Text to access your post's HTML editor and paste the embed code.

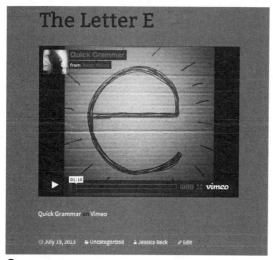

J A published post containing an embedded video.

Putting It All Together

1. **Experiment with your Media Library.** Using the Media Library, upload a few images. Try to resize and rotate an image.

2. **Create a photo gallery.** Can you use the images you already added through the Media Library? Can you add new images from the post editor while creating it?

3. **Add some multimedia content to a post.** Try embedding a video into a post. Can you add a video and a photo gallery to the same post? What options can you set when you add the video?

Managing Comments

One of the great things about a blog is the ability for readers to respond to and interact with both the author and other readers. How do they do this? By commenting, of course!

Comments are enabled by default on a new WordPress blog, but you can turn them off globally or on a per-post level if you want to keep interaction to a minimum. You can also enable comments on static pages.

This chapter will show you how to manage comments on your blog. We'll also show you how to identify and deal with spam, and we'll walk you through the process of setting up Akismet, a popular spam filter created by the same folks who brought you WordPress.

Enabling and Disabling Comments

You can control who is permitted to comment on your posts and pages. You can exercise that control by setting commenting privileges on each post or by globally tweaking the settings for your entire site.

To configure comment settings for your site:

1. Click Settings in the sidebar, and then click Discussion to open the Discussion Settings screen Ⓐ.

Ⓐ The Discussion Settings screen is where you configure the way your site handles comments.

2. Toggle the check boxes to activate or deactivate discussion settings for your site. The available options are as follows:

Default Article Settings: This section lets you decide whether readers are allowed to post comments. Also, you can choose to notify other blogs when you have linked to them in a post, and you can be notified each time another blog links to you—notifications that are also known as trackbacks and pingbacks, respectively **B**.

Other Comment Settings: Here's where you can fine-tune the way you handle comments on your site. You can require readers to fill out their names and email addresses before they are allowed to post; restrict comments to those who are registered and logged in to your site; set the amount of time a post will be open for comments (closing comments after two weeks, for example, to minimize spam); enable readers to have discussions using threaded comments; and choose when to break popular discussions into multiple pages and whether to display older or newer comments first **C**.

continues on next page

Default article settings	☑ Attempt to notify any blogs linked to from the article
	☑ Allow link notifications from other blogs (pingbacks and trackbacks)
	☑ Allow people to post comments on new articles
	(These settings may be overridden for individual articles.)

B Set your default article settings here. You can override these settings on individual posts.

Other comment settings	☑ Comment author must fill out name and e-mail
	☐ Users must be registered and logged in to comment
	☐ Automatically close comments on articles older than 14 days
	☑ Enable threaded (nested) comments 5 ▾ levels deep
	☐ Break comments into pages with 50 top level comments per page and the last ▾ page displayed by default
	Comments should be displayed with the older ▾ comments at the top of each page

C Choose how and when comments are displayed in this section.

Email Me Whenever: You can choose to be notified when a comment is posted or held for moderation **D**.

Before A Comment Appears: These options let you automatically hold comments until an administrator has approved them or automatically approve comments from a reader who has been previously approved **E**.

Comment Moderation: This section lets you specify limits on links and require moderation for comments containing certain words or phrases **F**.

| E-mail me whenever | ☑ Anyone posts a comment |
| | ☑ A comment is held for moderation |

D Set your notification preferences here.

| Before a comment appears | ☐ An administrator must always approve the comment |
| | ☑ Comment author must have a previously approved comment |

E If you don't want comments from unknown users to go live right away, you can hold them until an administrator has approved them.

Comment Moderation	Hold a comment in the queue if it contains 2 or more links. (A common characteristic of comment spam is a large number of hyperlinks.)
	When a comment contains any of these words in its content, name, URL, e-mail, or IP, it will be held in the moderation queue. One word or IP per line. It will match inside words, so "press" will match "WordPress".
	dating lottery singles

F If you enter keywords in this section, comments containing the keywords will automatically be held for moderation.

Comment Blacklist: You can automatically flag as spam comments that contain certain words. This option is similar to Comment Moderation but will send blacklisted comments straight to the spam folder rather than holding them for approval **G**.

Avatars: User pictures, or *avatars*, are an optional way for your readers to personalize their posts, and you can enable or disable them here. You can also choose a default for those who do not have an avatar **H**.

Comment Blacklist	When a comment contains any of these words in its content, name, URL, e-mail, or IP, it will be marked as spam. One word or IP per line. It will match inside words, so "press" will match "WordPress".
	Viagra
	hacker

G Comments containing any words or phrases entered in this section will automatically be flagged as spam, so choose keywords wisely!

Avatars

An avatar is an image that follows you from weblog to weblog appearing beside your name when you comment on avatar enabled sites. Here you can enable the display of avatars for people who comment on your site.

Avatar Display	☑ Show Avatars
Maximum Rating	◉ G — Suitable for all audiences
	○ PG — Possibly offensive, usually for audiences 13 and above
	○ R — Intended for adult audiences above 17
	○ X — Even more mature than above
Default Avatar	For users without a custom avatar of their own, you can either display a generic logo or a generated one based on their e-mail address.
	◉ Mystery Man
	○ Blank
	○ Gravatar Logo
	○ Identicon (Generated)
	○ Wavatar (Generated)
	○ MonsterID (Generated)
	○ Retro (Generated)

H Choose your default avatar settings here.

To configure comment settings on an individual post or page:

1. After writing a post or page (or from the Edit screen), expand the screen options pane, and ensure that the Discussion box is checked ⓘ.

2. Scroll down to the Discussion box, and toggle the check boxes to allow (or disallow) comments or trackbacks and pingbacks ⓙ.

TIP If you don't see the Discussion box, click Screen Options and select the check box next to Discussion.

Get a User Avatar with Gravatar

One of the most popular avatar-hosting services is Gravatar. It's owned by Automattic, the company behind WordPress, so it's compatible with both WordPress.com blogs and self-hosted WordPress sites.

If you have a WordPress.com login, you can use it to log in to the Gravatar service. From there you can set up a default avatar that will be associated with your email address. You can add more email addresses and assign images to each one. For example, you may want to use one avatar for your work email and another for your personal email addresses.

Find out more and sign up at http://en.gravatar.com.

ⓘ Toggle the screen options you wish to see.

Discussion

☑ Allow comments.
☑ Allow trackbacks and pingbacks on this page.

ⓙ You can override your default comment settings on a per-post basis by toggling these check boxes on a post or page.

A The Recent Comments widget on the WordPress Dashboard.

B You can approve, flag, edit, delete, or reply to a comment right from the Dashboard.

C Replying to a comment from the Dashboard.

Moderating Comments

Once you've received a few comments, you may find that they're not all legitimate. That's where moderation comes in. You can approve, delete, and mark comments as spam to keep your discussions on track. You can also choose to hold new comments in the moderation queue for review before they go live on your site.

To moderate a new comment from the dashboard:

1. Log in to your WordPress site to access the Recent Comments dashboard widget, which lists the newest comments on your posts **A**.

2. Hover over a comment in the list to access a simple menu that will let you moderate the comment right from the Dashboard **B**.

3. Use the tools to modify a comment's approval setting, edit it, flag it as spam, or delete it. You can also click the Reply link to submit a reply to the comment **C**.

To edit or approve comments:

1. Click Comments in the left sidebar to view a list of comments **D**.

   If you have pending comments awaiting moderation, you will see a number in the left sidebar next to Comments **E**.

2. Click the Pending link on the Edit Comments screen to view the pending comments **F**.

3. Hover over a pending comment to access the menu of options. You can approve, mark as spam, delete, edit, make quick edits, or reply to the comment.

4. To make quick edits to a comment in the comment list, hover over the one you wish to modify and click Quick Edit **G**.

   The Quick Edit feature is similar to the one for posts and pages in that it gives you a streamlined version of the regular editor so that you can quickly make a change **H**.

D Click Comments in the left sidebar to access your comments.

E If you have comments awaiting moderation, you will see a number next to the Comments link in the sidebar.

F Your pending comments are comments that require action before they can be posted on your site.

G To make quick edits to a comment, hover over it and choose Quick Edit.

H The Quick Edit screen is a pared-down version of the regular comment editor.

⓵ You can set a comment's status as well as edit its content from the comment editor.

One thought on "Astoria"

July 21, 2013 at 5:22 am   ✎ Edit

What great photos, a wonderful time was definitely had!

Site Administrator   ↳ Reply

⓳ Approved comments are published on your site.

5. For a more in-depth editing experience, click Edit in the list of options under the comment to open the Edit Comment screen. This screen allows you to edit the comment's content, just like Quick Edit, but it also lets you set the comment's status **⓵**.

6. After you have made any changes you need to make, click Update to save your changes.

If approved, comments are displayed on your site along with posts **⓳**.

How to Spot Spam

Spam is the colloquial term for unsolicited and unwelcome messages aimed at an individual or a Web site, and unfortunately, blogs get their fair share of spam disguised as comments. Some spam messages are easy to spot, whereas others might be confused for actual replies.

Here are some signs that a message is spam:

- **Multiple consecutive comments**. People rarely respond to their own comments, but spammers often do.
- **Keyword-heavy comments**. If a comment uses lots of keywords or a list of keywords, it's probably spam.
- **Links in comments**. A link doesn't automatically mean that a comment is spam, but spammers often include links to drive traffic to other sites.
- **Nonsensical or unrelated comments**. A reply of "Great article, lots of good information" may seem legitimate, but if it doesn't directly relate to the post it's responding to, it may be spam.

Fighting Spam with Akismet

Many plug-Ins are available to fight comment spam. One of the most popular is Akismet, a spam fighter that comes bundled with each WordPress installation. Created by Automattic, the company behind WordPress, Akismet is easy to set up and is free of charge for personal blogs. (Commercial and nonpersonal sites pay a small monthly or annual fee.)

To set up Akismet, you will need to get an API key from the Akismet site.

A Click Plugins to begin the process of activating the Akismet plug-in.

To set up Akismet:

1. Click the Plugins link in the sidebar to view your available plug-ins in the Manage Plugins window **A**.

2. Click the Activate link under the listing for Akismet **B**.

3. Click the "Activate Your Akismet Account" button that appears near the top of the screen to access the Akismet plug-in site, where you can get an Akismet API key **C**.

☐ **Akismet**
[Activate] Edit I Delete

Used by millions, Akismet is quite possibly the best way in the world to **protect your blog from comment and trackback spam**. It keeps your site protected from spam even while you sleep. To get started: 1) Click the "Activate" link to the left of this description, 2) Sign up for an Akismet API key, and 3) Go to your Akismet configuration page, and save your API key.

Version 2.5.8 I By Automattic I Visit plugin site

B Click the Activate link to activate the Akismet plug-in.

Activate your Akismet account   Almost done - activate your account and say goodbye to comment spam.

C Once the Akismet plug-in has been activated, you will need an Akismet account and API key to make it work.

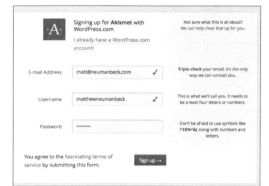

D Click the button to begin the sign-up process for the Akismet service.

E Sign up for an Akismet account.

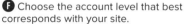

Akismet API key signup

Enter the URL of the site you'll use Akismet on, then choose a plan:

http://demo.wpvisualquickstart.com

Enterprise	Pro	Personal
$50/mo	$5/mo	$0-$120/yr
Multiple Site Access	Single-site access	Personal Blogs
For companies with multiple low traffic sites	For small non-personal sites or blogs	For non-business personal sites or blogs
SIGN UP	SIGN UP	SIGN UP

F Choose the account level that best corresponds with your site.

API key signup - It's easy

Sign up for an API key and wrestle your site's spam into submission

G Fill out the form to complete the sign-up process.

4. On the Akismet site, click the "Get An Akismet API Key" button **D**.

5. Fill in the "Signing Up for Akismet With WordPress.com" form to begin the sign-up process **E**.

6. Under Akismet API Key Signup, enter the URL of your site and choose the account level that corresponds best to the type of site you have. If your site is a personal site rather than a business or commercial site, click the Personal site link at the bottom of the screen **F**.

7. Enter your name and email address in the form on the left, and use the slider on the right to choose the amount you'd like to spend on Akismet (from $0 to $120/year) **G**.

If you choose to pay for Akismet or are signing up for a business plan, you will also need to enter your payment information here.

You will see a confirmation screen letting you know that your Akismet account is active **H**.

continues on next page

All Done!

Congratulations, you are the owner of a shiny new Akismet API key:

31d2ed00fe77

(we have also sent this API key to your email address)

H Your Akismet account is active. An email with more information will be sent to the address you used for the sign-up process.

8. Check your email for the message from Akismet that contains your API key **❶**. Copy the API key to your clipboard (Ctrl+C on Windows, Command+C on a Mac).

9. Return to your WordPress Dashboard and click Plugins in the sidebar. You will see a new option for Akismet Configuration **❶**. Click that link.

10. Paste your API key in the text box under the heading "Akismet API Key" **❸**.

Click Save Changes to continue.

Hi Matt Beck,

Thanks so much for using Akismet to help safeguard the web from spam.

Get Started

Your Akismet API key is: 31d2ed00fe77

Please keep this private, treat it like a password.

❶ In the confirmation email from Akismet, select the API key and copy it to your clipboard.

Akismet

Akismet eliminates the comment and trackback spam you get on your site. To use Akismet you may need to sign up for an API key. Click the button below to get started.

Create a new Akismet Key

I already have a key

❶ Click to access the Akismet Configuration screen.

Akismet

Akismet API Key
31d2ed00fe77

You must enter a valid Akismet API key here. If you need an API key, you can create one here

Save Changes

❸ Add your API key here, and click Save Changes.

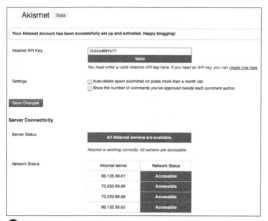

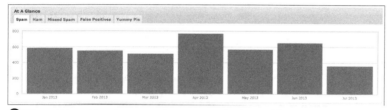

L Change Akismet's settings, and see the status of the Akismet servers.

11. Success! Akismet is now activated and ready to start catching spam comments.

    If you'd like to set some additional parameters, use the check boxes to choose to automatically delete spam on posts more than a month old or to show the number of previously approved comments next to each comment author **L**.

12. You will now see a link to your Akismet stats in the left sidebar menu under the Dashboard heading. Once your site has accrued some statistics, click that link to see a breakdown of the spam that has been caught on your site **M**.

M When Akismet has been running on your site for a while, you can view a detailed breakdown of your spam statistics.

How Does Akismet Work?

Akismet uses a unique algorithm combined with a community-created database to sort spam comments from legitimate comments. Once you've installed Akismet, each message you mark as spam is added to the community-created database, which helps the plug-in to identify similar comments. You can always visit your spam queue to be sure legitimate comments haven't been tagged as spam **N**.

	Author	Comment
☐		
☐	**Short-term investments** profit-day.ru/den-5yiy-pozitsil-ne-otkryivalis.ht... x SouthernVazguez64@aol.com 95.79.161.89	Submitted on 2013/07/20 at 11:57 pm Just desire to say your article is as astonishing. The clearness for your submit is just great and i could think you are knowledgeable on this subject. Well along with your permission allow me to clutch your RSS feed to keep up to date with approaching post. Thanks 1,000,000 and please continue the rewarding work.

N Comments in the spam queue.

Putting It All Together

1. **Change your comment settings.** How do you limit commenting to people who have registered on your site?

2. **Enable Gravatars.** What is a Gravatar? What displays if a user doesn't have a Gravatar?

3. **Set up Akismet.** Do you need to pay for this service if you're running a personal site? What if the Web site is for a business? How do you enable the Akismet plug-in on your site?

Getting Fancy
with Themes

So you want to make your theme a little less generic? Then this is the chapter for you! We'll walk you through the process of making modifications to your theme. In particular, we'll teach you how to use HTML and Cascading Style Sheets (CSS) to customize key aspects of your theme; how to add a favicon, the little icon that identifies a site in the bookmark bar of some browsers; and how to edit the functions.php file to add support for exciting WordPress attributes like featured images, custom backgrounds and headers, and custom menus.

Customizing Your Theme with CSS

With a little knowledge of CSS, you can make some major changes to the look and feel of your theme without touching the underlying structure. A *style sheet* is a CSS file that tells your browser how to display the site. All WordPress themes use a style sheet called style.css for the main CSS . Some themes include additional style sheets, as well. By making a few edits to a theme's style sheets, you can change text colors, background color, and font styles.

WordPress features a built-in editor that lets you edit your theme's style sheets and template files directly from your admin area. (You'll learn more about template files in Chapter 12, "Advanced Theme Development.") You can access the theme editor by going to Appearance > Editor. When you open the Edit Themes screen, the first template file that displays is your current theme's style sheet. If you need to open the style sheet after you've clicked on another template file, you can always find it at the bottom of the list of theme files in the Edit Themes sidebar.

It's important to note that style.css always starts with a *comment* (which can be any text located between /* and */ tags) that contains a block of metadata about the theme **B**. *Do not* delete this data! WordPress uses the metadata to identify the theme in the admin screen **C**.

TIP Changes you make to your theme's template files will take effect as soon as you save them. Directly editing a template file runs the risk of breaking your site. Always back up your theme before attempting any edits or changes!

A Any style sheets associated with your theme appear at the bottom of your template file list in the theme editor.

```
/*
Theme Name: Our Theme
Theme URI: http://www.wpvisualquickstart.com/our-theme
Description: A WordPress theme for the WordPress Visual QuickStart site
Author: Jessica Neuman Beck and Matt Beck
Author URI: http://www.couldbestudios.com
Tags: 2 column, simple, clean, widgets, fixed width
Version: 1.5

This theme has been designed as an example for WordPress Visual QuickStart.
*/
```

B Your theme's metadata, which is used to identify the theme in the WordPress admin area.

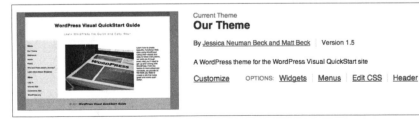

C A theme in the WordPress admin area, with the metadata providing such information as the theme title, author, and tags.

```
p {
color: #111;
}
```

D The style.css entry for text color.

To change text color with CSS:

1. Choose a color scheme for your site's text. You can choose colors for any text on your site, but important ones are main body text, links, headers, and footers.

2. Look at the style.css file in the theme editor, and find the entry for the default text color for your site **D**.

3. CSS colors are entered in hexadecimal format; a good online color-picking resource is www.colorschemer.com/online.html. Enter the hexadecimal color for your text, starting with a hash mark. It will look something like **color: #000000;**.

4. Find the other text you'd like to change, and repeat step 3.

5. Click Update File to save your changes.

TIP There are many online resources for choosing color schemes. Two that we like are Adobe's kuler (http://kuler.adobe.com) and COLOURLovers (www.colourlovers.com).

What Is CSS?

CSS (Cascading Style Sheets) assigns rules to sections of your markup. These rules define how your site appears to visitors. Keeping the actual content of your site separate from the presentation makes it easy for you to make cosmetic changes to your site without modifying any of your site's markup.

CSS works by using a selector to declare which existing markup element to affect, and then specifying rules that apply to that element. These rules are called a *declaration block*, and they're surrounded by brackets. Each declaration consists of a property, a colon (:), and a value. If you're using more than one declaration in your declaration block, each one ends with a semicolon (;).

For example, here is a paragraph in HTML:

<p>I am a paragraph.</p>

To modify the paragraph to display with a 10-pixel margin on all sides using CSS, you would type this into your CSS file:

```
p {
margin: 10px;
}
```

To change the background color with CSS:

1. Choose a background color that you'd like to use.

2. In the style.css file, find the **body** selector and look for the word **background** Ⓔ.

3. Replace the existing background color with the hexadecimal color of your choice.

4. Click Update File to save your changes.

> **TIP** Later in this chapter, we'll walk you through the process of adding custom background support to your theme. If your theme supports custom backgrounds, you can change the background color or even the image right in your admin area. For instructions on using custom backgrounds, check out Chapter 5, "Setting Up a WordPress Theme."

```
body {
        background:#aaa;
        margin:0;
        padding:0;
        font-family:"Helvetica Neue", Helvetica, Arial, sans-serif;
}
```

Ⓔ The style.css entry for background color.

```
font-family:"Helvetica Neue", Helvetica, Arial, sans-serif;
```

F Change fonts by adding to or changing the font names in the **font-family** declaration.

To change font style with CSS:

1. In the style.css file, find the font you'd like to change. The selector you're looking for will begin with **font-family F**.

2. Enter your font choice and note whether the font is serif or sans serif. The font listed first is the font that will attempt to be displayed first; if it cannot be displayed (for example, if a site visitor has an older computer that can't render your chosen font), the next listed font will be used as a backup. Separate each option with a comma, like this:

   font-family: Georgia,
   → **'Times New Roman', serif;**

3. Click Update File to save your changes.

To customize a menu item with CSS:

1. Go to Appearance > Menus to open the Edit Menus screen **G**.

2. Click the Screen Options tab at the top right.

continues on next page

Edit Menus	Manage Locations		Screen Options ▼	Help ▼

Select a menu to edit: Main Navigation (Navigation Menu) ▲▼ [Select] or create a new menu.

Pages ▼

Most Recent | View All | Search

☐ About Us
☐ Blog
☐ Home
☐ Sample Page
☐ Our Work
☐ Reference
  ☐ Our Theme

Menu Name: Main Navigation   [Save Menu]

Menu Structure

Drag each item into the order you prefer. Click the arrow on the right of the item to reveal additional configuration options.

Home	Custom ▼
Blog	Page ▼
About	Page ▼

G Open the Edit Menus screen, and click the Screen Options tab.

3. Under "Show advanced menu properties," check the box next to CSS Classes .

4. Scroll down to find the menu item you'd like to customize. Click the triangle to the right of the menu item's title to expand its options. In the CSS Classes box, enter a class selector for your menu item ❶.

5. Click Save Menu to update your menu.

6. Go to Appearance > Editor to access the style.css file.

7. Add an entry for your new CSS class ❶. Between the brackets, enter the modifiers for your menu item, like this:

```
.red {
   color: red;
   font-weight: bold;
}
```

8. Save the changes you have made to the style.css file.

9. On the front end of your site, notice that the menu item you customized now displays in the color red with a bold weight ❶.

Ⓗ Select the check box next to CSS Classes.

Ⓘ Add a CSS class name in the CSS Class box.

```
.red {
color: red;
font-weight:bold;
}
```

Ⓙ In your style.css file, add an entry for your new CSS class.

Ⓚ One menu item is now styled differently from the rest of your menu items.

WordPress Visual QuickSta

A A favicon on a tab in Google Chrome.

Adding a Favicon

A *favicon*, short for favorites icon, is a tiny 16-by-16-pixel graphic that appears next to your site's URL and title in the title bar on most browsers **A**. A favicon is often used for visual identification in a browser's bookmarks as well as in the address bar and on tabs.

Favicon files use the ICO file format, so be sure your graphics program supports that format before continuing.

TIP You can use an online favicon generator, such as Favikon (http://favikon.com), to convert an existing image to a favicon.

To add a favicon to your theme:

1. Using a graphics program such as Adobe Photoshop, create a 16-by-16-pixel image.

2. Save the file as an ICO file with the name favicon.ico.

3. Upload the favicon.ico file to your current theme's main folder **B**.

continues on next page

Name ▲	Size	Date
author.php	1 KB	2/26/11 5:34 PM
footer.php	385 B	8/21/10 1:41 PM
functions.php	910 B	8/2/10 12:07 PM
header.php	2 KB	2/26/11 4:06 PM
index.php	1 KB	2/26/11 5:25 PM
page.php	919 B	6/10/10 1:02 PM
screenshot.jpg	482 KB	6/10/10 1:02 PM
sidebar.php	304 B	6/10/10 1:02 PM
single.php	1 KB	2/26/11 5:28 PM
style.css	4 KB	2/26/11 5:31 PM
favicon.ico		

B Upload your favicon to the main folder of your current theme.

4. In the theme editor, open the header.php file.

5. Find the line that begins with `<link rel="shortcut icon"` and ends with `/favicon.ico" />`. Overwrite it, or (if no favicon has been previously specified) add the following code below the `<head>` HTML tag **C**:

```
<link rel="shortcut icon"
→href="<?php

bloginfo('stylesheet_
→directory'); ?>/favicon.ico" />
```

6. Click Update File to save your changes. Your new favicon will now display next to your URL in most browsers.

Our Theme: Header (header.php)

```
<!DOCTYPE html PUBLIC "-//W3C//DTD XHTML 1.0 Transitional//EN"
    "http://www.w3.org/TR/xhtml1/DTD/xhtml1-transitional.dtd">

<html xmlns="http://www.w3.org/1999/xhtml" xml:lang="en" lang="en">
<head>
<link rel="shortcut icon" href="<?php bloginfo('stylesheet_directory'); ?>/favicon.ico" />
```

C Enter the favicon code in your header.php file.

Templates

Author Template
(author.php)

Footer
(footer.php)

Theme Functions
(functions.php)

Header
(header.php)

Main Index Template
(index.php)

Sub Page List Page Template
(list.php)

Page Template
(page.php)

Portfolio Page Template
(portfolio.php)

Sidebar
(sidebar.php)

Single Post
(single.php)

Styles

Stylesheet
(style.css)

Ⓐ You'll find the functions.php file in your list of templates on the Edit Themes screen.

Editing the Functions File

The functions.php file is the brains of a WordPress theme. By adding some simple code snippets, you can make some big changes to the way your theme works.

You can locate your functions.php file in the list of templates in the Edit Themes screen Ⓐ. It's always a good idea to save a backup of your original functions.php file in case you make a change that doesn't work the way you anticipated.

In this section, you will be adding featured image support, which will allow you to associate an image with a post. You'll add support for custom headers, which will let you add and change your header image from your admin area, and custom background support so that you can also add and change your background image from the admin area. Finally, you'll add custom menu support.

To add featured image support:

1. Open the functions.php file in the Edit Themes screen.

2. After the opening **<?php**, add the following code **B**:

   ```
   if (function_exists('add_theme_
   →support')) {
   
   add_theme_support('post-
   →thumbnails');
   
   }
   ```

3. Click Update File to save your changes.

   Your theme now supports featured images. When you open a new post, you will see the option to add a featured image at the bottom of the right sidebar column **C**.

   TIP To add multiple featured image sizes and for more information on integrating featured images into your theme, visit http://codex.wordpress.org/Post_Thumbnails.

```
// Add support for Featured Images
if (function_exists('add_theme_support')) {
    add_theme_support('post-thumbnails');
}
```

B Enter the code to add featured image support to your theme.

C Featured Images are now supported.

```
<?php

add_custom_background();
```

 **D** Add the code to use custom backgrounds on your site.

E The Background link in the Appearance menu means your theme supports custom backgrounds.

To add custom background support:

1. Open the functions.php file in the Edit Themes screen.

2. After the opening **<?php**, add the following code **D**:

   add_custom_background();

3. Click Update File to save your changes.

   Your theme now supports custom backgrounds. Click Appearance to see the new Background link in the sidebar menu **E**.

To add custom header support:

1. Open the functions.php file in the Edit Themes screen.

2. After the opening **<?php**, add the following code **F**:

   ```
   define( 'HEADER_IMAGE', '
   →%s/images/header.jpg' );
   →// The default header located
   →in themes folder

   define( 'HEADER_IMAGE_WIDTH',
   → apply_filters( '', 845 ) );
   →// Width of header

   define( 'HEADER_IMAGE_HEIGHT',
   → apply_filters( '', 365 ) );
   →// Height of header

   define( 'NO_HEADER_TEXT', true );

   add_custom_image_header( '',
   → 'admin_header_style' ); // This
   → Enables the Appearance > Header

   // Following Code is for Styling
   → the Admin Side

   if ( ! function_exists( 'admin_
   → header_style' ) ) :

   function admin_header_style() {
   ?>

   <style type="text/css">
   ```

continues on next page

```
#headimg {

height: <?php echo HEADER_IMAGE_
→ HEIGHT; ?>px;

width: <?php echo HEADER_IMAGE_
→ WIDTH; ?>px;

}

#headimg h1, #headimg #desc {

display: none;

}

</style>

<?php

}

endif;
```

3. Find the **HEADER_IMAGE_WIDTH** block of code, and change the width. In our example, the header is 845 pixels wide; change the 845 to the pixel width you'd like to use for your site:

```
define( 'HEADER_IMAGE_WIDTH',
→ apply_filters( '', 845 ) );
→// Width of header
```

```
define( 'HEADER_IMAGE', '%s/images/header.png' ); // The default header located in themes folder
define( 'HEADER_IMAGE_WIDTH', apply_filters( '', 845 ) ); // Width of header
define( 'HEADER_IMAGE_HEIGHT', apply_filters( '', 365 ) ); // Height of header
define( 'NO_HEADER_TEXT', true );
add_custom_image_header( '', 'admin_header_style' ); // This Enables the Appearance > Header
// Following Code is for Styling the Admin Side
if ( ! function_exists( 'admin_header_style' ) ) :
function admin_header_style() {
?>
<style type="text/css">
#headimg {
height: <?php echo HEADER_IMAGE_HEIGHT; ?>px;
width: <?php echo HEADER_IMAGE_WIDTH; ?>px;
}
#headimg h1, #headimg #desc {
display: none;
}
</style>
<?php
}
endif;
```

F Add this whole block of code to your functions.php file to enable custom header support.

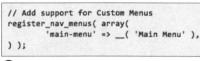

G You can now click Header in the Appearance menu to add a custom header to your site.

```
// Add support for Custom Menus
register_nav_menus( array(
        'main-menu' => __( 'Main Menu' ),
) );
```

H Add the code to enable your site to handle custom menus.

I After the code is added, you can create custom menus by clicking the Menus link.

4. Find the **HEADER_IMAGE_HEIGHT** block of code, and change the height. In our example, the header is 365 pixels tall; change the 365 to the pixel height you'd like to use for your site:

```
define( 'HEADER_IMAGE_HEIGHT',
→ apply_filters( '', 365 ) );
→// Height of header
```

5. Click Update File to save your changes to the functions.php file.

6. Using the dimensions you have specified, create and save a default header image using a graphics program such as Photoshop. Save it as a JPEG file with the name header.jpg, and upload it to your theme's images folder.

7. In your WordPress Dashboard, click Appearance and you will see that the Header link now appears in the menu **G**.

To add custom menu support:

1. Open the functions.php file in the Edit Themes screen.

2. After the opening **<?php**, add the following code **H**:

```
register_nav_menus( array(

'main-menu' => __( 'Main Menu' ),

) );
```

3. Click Update File to save your changes.

You will see the new link to Menus in your Appearance sidebar **I**.

TIP To add support for multiple menus and for more information on integrating custom menus into your theme, visit http://codex.wordpress.org/Navigation_Menus.

Putting It All Together

1. **Open your style.css file.** What sorts of changes can be made using only this file?

2. **Change the color of your site's text.** How do you specify a new text color?

3. **Create a favicon.** In what format must you save this file? How do you add a link to your new favicon to your theme?

4. **Open your functions.php file.** Be sure to make a backup of your original file. What functions are already there? Where do you add the code for a new function?

5. **Add custom background support to your theme.** Where do you add the code to support custom backgrounds? What is added to the Appearance menu after you click Update File?

Advanced Theme Development

In this chapter, you'll learn to design and build a simple theme from scratch. Theme building in WordPress requires a strong knowledge of Web design, HTML/ XHTML, CSS, and PHP. Novice users need not apply! For designers and developers, however, building your own theme offers unparalleled flexibility and power, especially when compared to using or modifying a prebuilt theme.

Anatomy of a WordPress Theme

Your theme may appear as one cohesive whole, but many different pieces go into each page of a site **A**.

Themes are generally made up of three types of files: style sheets, template files, and (optionally) a function file. Most themes also include some background images and a screen shot image.

The minimum requirements to build a functional WordPress site are a style sheet named style.css and an index.php template file. To create a dynamic, fully featured theme, you will need to set up several more template files. All of these go into your theme's directory.

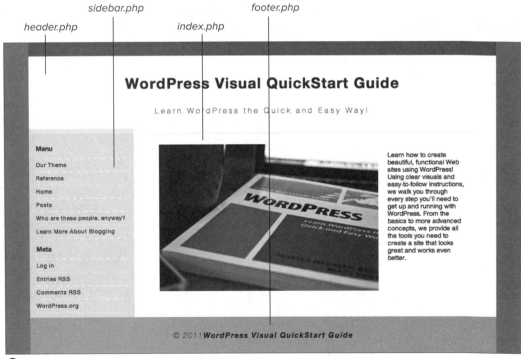

header.php   *sidebar.php*   *index.php*   *footer.php*

WordPress Visual QuickStart Guide

Learn WordPress the Quick and Easy Way!

Menu

Our Theme

Reference

Home

Posts

Who are these people, anyway?

Learn More About Blogging

Meta

Log in

Entries RSS

Comments RSS

WordPress.org

Learn how to create beautiful, functional Web sites using WordPress! Using clear visuals and easy-to-follow instructions, we walk you through every step you'll need to get up and running with WordPress. From the basics to more advanced concepts, we provide all the tools you need to create a site that looks great and works even better.

© 2011 *WordPress Visual QuickStart Guide*

A The front page of this site is composed of several files: header.php, sidebar.php, index.php, and footer.php.

Theme-Building Shortcuts: Frameworks

Frameworks are a great way to save time when building a new theme, because the site's basic structure is built right in. Numerous frameworks are available, and many of them are created just for WordPress.

One popular framework is the Roots Theme, which includes several options that make the development process easy. It includes some minimal graphic styles and lots of layout options. You can learn more about the Roots Theme at www.rootstheme.com.

The Roots Theme also makes use of Blueprint, a CSS framework that gives you a head start on common styling elements like typography, column widths, and cross-browser compatibility. You can familiarize yourself with the Blueprint framework at www.blueprintcss.org.

Another popular framework is the Underscores starter theme, which was developed by Automattic (the folks behind WordPress). This theme is fully compatible with the latest version of WordPress and includes lots of optional functions and templates. You can find out more about the Underscores theme at http://underscores.me.

If you do not include certain files (such as comments.php), WordPress will pull the default versions into your site. If you find that you need to make changes to the parts of your site that are generated by default templates, simply create your own template files and WordPress will automatically use those instead.

In building your theme, it's best to use your text editor to edit theme files. Once you have a basic theme working, you can install it on your site and make changes using the built-in theme editor in WordPress.

TIP Theme template files are located in the WordPress install directory called /wp-content/themes/. To create a new directory for your theme, you will add a new folder to the /wp-content/themes/ directory. For example, if your theme is called Our Theme, you will create a folder called our-theme. The path to your theme will be /wp-content/themes/our-theme/.

Building a Theme from Scratch

If you've always wanted to build your own theme, this is the section for you! In the following task, you'll walk through the process of creating a basic WordPress theme from start to finish.

TIP To get a better grasp of how all these code snippets go together, download the complete working example theme from our site at http://wpvisualquickstart.com/our-theme.zip. It's the same theme used on the site and discussed in this book.

TIP For more information on themes and how to build them, check out Theme Development on the WordPress Codex: http://codex.wordpress.org/Theme_Development.

A The wp-content/themes directory contains subdirectories for each theme you have installed.

B A basic theme could consist of just style.css and index.php and still function correctly.

To create a basic blank theme:

1. Using your FTP client, create a new directory for your theme in your WordPress site's /wp-content/themes directory **A**. Name this directory after your new theme, replacing any spaces with dashes or underscores—/wp-content/themes/our-theme, for example.

2. Create a new file called index.php, and upload it to the directory you just created.

3. Repeat the process to create header. php, sidebar.php, footer.php, functions. php, and style.css files, and upload them to the same place **B**.

4. Using your favorite text editor, such as TextMate for the Mac or TextPad on Windows, open your style.css file and add the following required comment section at the top **C**:

```
/*

Theme Name: Our Theme

Theme URI: http://www.
→ wpvisualquickstart.com/
→ our-theme

Description: A WordPress theme
→ for the WordPress Visual
→ QuickStart site

Author: Jessica Neuman Beck and
→ Matt Beck

Author URI: http://www.
→ couldbestudios.com

Tags: 2 column, simple, clean,
→ widgets, fixed width

Version: 1.0


This theme has been designed as
→ an example for WordPress Visual
→ QuickStart.

*/
```

You will notice that the comment section begins and ends with **/*** and ***/**. Everything between those symbols is considered a comment and is ignored by browsers looking for style information.

The information in this particular comment is used by WordPress to generate the information used on the theme selection screen (Appearance > Themes).

continues on next page

```
1   /*
2   Theme Name: Our Theme
3   Theme URI: http://www.wpvisualquickstart.com/our-theme
4   Description: A WordPress theme for the WordPress Visual QuickStart site
5   Author: Jessica Neuman Beck and Matt Beck
6   Author URI: http://www.couldbestudios.com
7   Tags: 2 column, simple, clean, widgets, fixed width
8   Version: 1.0
9
10  This theme has been designed as an example for WordPress Visual QuickStart.
11  */
```

C The style.css file holds some important data in a required comment block.

This comment contains several variables followed by a colon and a value. The required variables are **Theme Name**, **Theme URI**, **Description**, **Author,** and **Author URI**.

Optional variables are **Tags**, **Template**, and **Version**. If you do not wish to use one of the optional variables, just leave it out completely.

5. After listing the variables in the comment block, enter any additional text you'd like to include, such as licensing information.

   For example, in the previous code, the line **This theme has been designed as an example for WordPress Visual QuickStart** is the type of additional text you might enter in this section. Just make sure you place the text after the required variables and before the final ***/** symbol.

6. Save and close your style.css file and upload it to your theme's directory.

   The data in the comment block, and a screen shot if you have provided one (see the following tip for instructions on including a screen shot), will be displayed in the WordPress admin area in the Themes screen **D**. You can access this screen by clicking Appearance in the admin sidebar menu and then clicking Themes.

7. Open the header.php file in your text editor. This is the file that will control the information your visitors will see at the top of your Web site; it will also contain meta-information that is not displayed on your site but that conveys important information to browsers (such as where to find other template files).

8. Add a document type (**DOCTYPE**) to your header.php file. This tells the browser how to interpret the XHTML code. For our theme, we used the following:

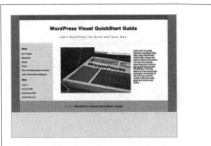

Our Theme 1.0 by Jessica Neuman Beck and Matt Beck

A WordPress theme for the WordPress Visual QuickStart site

Activate | Preview | Delete

All of this theme's files are located in `/themes/our-theme` .

Tags: 2 column, simple, clean, widgets, fixed width

D The data from the comment block in style.css is displayed in the Themes screen.

```
<!DOCTYPE html PUBLIC "-//W3C//
→ DTD XHTML 1.0 Transitional//EN"
→ "http://www.w3.org/TR/xhtml1/
→ DTD/xhtml1-transitional.dtd">
```

You can find more information on doctypes for WordPress at http://codex .wordpress.org/HTML_to_XHTML.

9. After the **DOCTYPE** declaration, add an opening **<html>** tag (you will close this in the footer.php file) and begin entering your theme's meta-information **E**. This information goes between **<head>** and **</head>** tags, which tells the browser that the information is to be processed before the main body of the Web site (which comes next).

The most important meta tag to include is the link to the style sheet. Without this, your CSS will not be applied to your theme. Add a link to your style sheet like this:

```
<link rel="stylesheet"
→ type="text/css" media="all"
→ href="<?php bloginfo(
→ 'stylesheet_url' ); ?>" />
```

continues on next page

```
1   <!DOCTYPE html PUBLIC "-//W3C//DTD XHTML 1.0 Transitional//EN" "http://www.w3.org/TR/xhtml1/DTD/
    xhtml1-transitional.dtd">
2   <html <?php language_attributes(); ?>>
3   <head>
4       <meta charset="<?php bloginfo( 'charset' ); ?>" />
5       <title>
6           <?php bloginfo('name'); ?> <?php wp_title(); ?>
7       </title>
8
9       <link rel="profile" href="http://gmpg.org/xfn/11" />
10      <link rel="stylesheet" type="text/css" media="all" href="<?php bloginfo( 'stylesheet_url' ); ?
>" />
11      <link rel="pingback" href="<?php bloginfo( 'pingback_url' ); ?>" />
12
13      <?php wp_head(); ?>
14  </head>
15  <body <?php body_class(); ?>>
16      <div id="page">
17          <div id="header">
18              <h1><a href="<?php echo esc_url( home_url( '/' ) ); ?>" title="<?php echo
    esc_attr( get_bloginfo( 'name', 'display' ) ); ?>" rel="home"><?php bloginfo( 'name' ); ?></a></h1>
19              <h4><?php bloginfo('description'); ?></h4>
20          </div>
```

E The header.php file contains some important information for browsers.

Here are some other meta tags you may want to add to your header.php file:

```
<meta charset="<?php bloginfo(
→ 'charset' ); ?>" />
```

This sets the character set for your site, which you have specified in the Settings > Reading Settings section of the admin area.

```
<title> <?php bloginfo('name');
→ ?> <?php wp_title(); ?>
→ </title>
```

This `<title>` tag uses shortcode to pull in the title of your site from the Settings section of your WordPress admin area. This title displays in the title area of your browser window.

```
<meta name="description"
→ content="<?php bloginfo
→ ('description'); ?>"/>
```

This is the description for your site, and it uses WordPress shortcode to pull the description directly from the Settings section of your WordPress admin area.

10. Add one more WordPress-specific tag:

```
<?php wp_head(); ?>
```

This is called a theme hook, and it allows plug-ins to display information directly in certain sections of your theme. Without this theme hook, some plug-ins may not work.

11. After your meta information, make sure you add a closing `</head>` tag after this theme hook.

12. After the final closing `</head>` tag, add an opening `<body>` tag (you will close this tag in the footer.php file). You may want to enclose the main content area of your site in an additional `<div id="page">` tag, which will allow you to set a width for your content. This tag will also be closed in the footer.php file.

13. Now you can add the code that will display the header of your site, such as the site's name. Here's an example:

```
<div id="header">

<h1><a href="<?php echo esc_url
→ ( home_url( '/' ) ); ?>"
→ title="<?php echo esc_attr(
→ get_bloginfo( 'name', 'display'
→ ) ); ?>" rel="home"><?php
→ bloginfo( 'name' ); ?></a></h1>

</div>
```

14. Save your header.php file and upload it to your theme's directory.

15. Open the index.php file and add the XHTML structure for the main portion of your site, including the WordPress Loop (described later in this chapter, in the "Using the Loop" section) **F**. The index. php file provides the primary structure for your site. Make sure you include the shortcode that will pull in the header, sidebar, and footer files.

continues on next page

```
1   <?php get_header();?>
2   <?php get_sidebar(); ?>
3   <div id="content">
4   <!--START THE LOOP-->
5       <?php if(have_posts()) : while(have_posts()) : the_post(); ?>
6       <div class="entry">
7           <h2><a href="<?php the_permalink(); ?>"><?php the_title(); ?></a></h2>
8           <div class="entry-body">
9           <?php the_content(); ?>
10              <div class="post-metadata">
11                  <span class="author">By <?php the_author_posts_link(); ?></span>
12                  <span class="date"><?php the_time('F j6, Y'); ?></span>
13                  <span class="categories">See more in: <?php the_category(' &raquo; '); ?></span>
14              </div>
15              </div>
16      </div>
17          <?php endwhile; else: ?>
18      <p><?php _e('Sorry, no posts matched your criteria.'); ?></p>
19          <?php endif; ?>
20  <!--END THE LOOP-->
21  </div>
22  <?php get_footer(); ?>
```

F Include the WordPress loop as well as the shortcode to pull your header, sidebar, and footer files into your index.php file.

16. Save and close your index.php file. Upload it to your template directory.

17. Open your sidebar.php file, and add the following code to display widgets in your sidebar:

```
<div id="sidebar">

<?php dynamic_sidebar( 'primary'
↪ ); ?>

</div>
```

If you want to display additional information or code in your sidebar that isn't available via widgets, you may enter it here. To display your information before your widgets, enter it just below the opening **<div>**; to display it after your widgets, enter your information just above the final closing **</div>**.

18. Save and close your sidebar.php file. Upload it to your theme directory.

19. Open your functions.php file, and add the following code to register your widgetized sidebar:

```php
<?php
add_action( 'widgets_init',
→ 'my_sidebar' );
function my_sidebar() {
/* Register the 'primary'
→ sidebar. */
register_sidebar(
array(
    'id' => 'primary',
    'name' => -( 'Primary' ),
    'description' => -( 'This is
    → the primary sidebar.' ),
    'before_widget' => '<div

    → id="%1$s" class="widget
    → %2$s">',
    'after_widget' => '</div>',
    'before_title' => '<h3
    → class="widget-title">',
    'after_title' => '</h3>'
    )
);
}
?>
```

20. Save and close your functions.php file. Upload it to your theme directory.

continues on next page

21. Open the footer.php file, and enter the information you want to appear in your site's footer. This often includes copyright and design information, as in this example:

```
<div id="footer>

<cite>

&copy; <?php echo date
  → ('Y'); ?><a href="<?php
  → bloginfo('url');?><?php
  → bloginfo('name'); ?></a>

</cite>

</div>
```

22. At the end of your footer file, close the `<div id="page">` tag you opened in the header.php file. Add the theme hook `<?php wp_footer(); ?>` to enable plug-in support. Finally, close the `<body>` and `<html>` tags **G**. Make sure the last lines of your footer.php file include this code:

```
</body>

</html>
```

23. Save and close your footer.php file. Upload it to your theme directory.

```
1  <div id="footer">
2      <cite>
3      &copy; <?php echo date('Y'); ?><a href="<?php bloginfo('url');?>"><?php bloginfo('name'); ?></a>
4      </cite>
5  </div>
6  <?php wp_footer(); ?>
7  </div>
8  </body>
9  </html>
```

G Close the `<body>` and `<html>` tags in your footer.php file.

TIP You can include an image of your finished theme to display on the WordPress Themes page in your admin area by uploading a **PNG** or **JPEG** file called "screenshot" to your theme's directory.

TIP The theme described in this section includes only a few of the template files used to create our full theme. A detailed walkthrough demonstrating how to build a theme with file-by-file breakdowns and full code samples is available at www. wpvisualquickstart.com/reference/ theme-building.

TIP WordPress will use the default versions of any templates you leave out. Read on to learn about working with template files and to find out about additional templates you may want to include in your theme.

Working with Template Files

Template files are where all of the magic happens in your theme. These files pull data from your site's database and generate the HTML that will be displayed on your site.

WordPress generates dynamic content by using two different types of templates:

- Those that generate a specific display—such as single.php, which is used to display a single blog post—are essentially a replacement for the index.php file.

- Those that are included in other templates—such as header.php, sidebar.php, and footer.php—need to be placed in another template in order to function, like a piece in a jigsaw puzzle.

You can also create your own templates when building a theme, even if they are not automatically recognized in the WordPress template hierarchy. Instead of using a WordPress template tag to include the file, you can use the **php include()** function with the **TEMPLATEPATH** variable to do so:

```php
<?php include (TEMPLATEPATH . '/
→ templatename.php'); ?>
```

TIP You can find more information about the WordPress template files at www.wpvisualquickstart.com/reference/wordpress-templates.

TIP See "Template Hierarchy" later in this chapter to learn which templates are displayed in what order.

WordPress Template Files

Although you can create a functional site using only the style.css and index.php files, WordPress gives you the option of using many different templates. To make doing so easy, WordPress automatically recognizes several templates, including:

- Page Not Found Template (404.php)
- Archive Template (archive.php)
- Archive Index Template (archives.php)
- Attachment Template (attachment.php)
- Author Page Template (author.php)
- Category Template (category.php)
- Comments Template (comments.php)
- Date/Time Template (date.php)
- Footer Template (footer.php)
- Front Page Template (front-page. php); this can be used with either a static front page or a standard posts front page
- Header Template (header.php)
- Home Template (home.php); this is used only if you have a static front page
- Image Template (image.php)
- Links Template (links.php)
- Main (Default) Template (index.php)
- Page Template (page.php)
- Post Template (single.php)
- Search Form (searchform.php)
- Search Page Template (search.php)
- Sidebar Template (sidebar.php)
- Tags Template (tag.php)
- Taxonomy Template (taxonomy.php)

Template Hierarchy

Most of the available WordPress templates are not mandatory, and WordPress provides a hierarchy to show the order in which it looks for specific templates when displaying content.

For example, if your theme includes a home.php template, WordPress will use that template to display your content to viewers of your site's home page. But if the home.php template isn't included in your theme, WordPress will display your home page content using the index.php template instead.

A more complicated example involves tag display. If you have a tag.php template file, WordPress will use that file when someone clicks on one of your tags. If you don't have a tag.php file, WordPress will use the archive.php file to display your tagged posts. If you don't have an archive.php file either, WordPress will use the index.php template to display the content.

You can almost always assign even more fine-grained control to individual pages, categories, tags, or the like by creating a template specific to it. For instance, using our tag example earlier, if you wanted to assign a special template to everything that is tagged "breakfast," you would create a template named tag-breakfast.php. In the template hierarchy, the more specific template always takes precedence

TIP See a full list of template hierarchy at http://codex.wordpress.org/Template_Hierarchy.

Working with Template Tags

Template tags are PHP functions that pull information from the database for your WordPress site and display it or make it available for you to manipulate with PHP when it is used in your templates.

Many of the template tags accept parameters or modifiers that let you manipulate the information that is pulled from the database and/or change the output of the function. The parameters accepted (if any) vary from tag to tag.

There are two ways that template tags accept parameters: either by accepting standard PHP function parameters (strings, arrays, and the like) or with a query-string style parameter.

To use a template tag with standard PHP parameters:

1. Open your header.php file in a text editor or in the Edit Themes screen of your WordPress admin.

2. Find the `bloginfo` tag.

3. Refer to the list of available parameters for the `bloginfo` tag on the WordPress Codex at http://codex.wordpress.org/Template_Tags/bloginfo to see a full list of options.

   The `bloginfo` tag can accept a single string as a parameter—for example, `<?php bloginfo('description'); ?>`— which will output the description of your site as specified in the General Settings section of your admin area.

4. Enter your chosen parameter in the parentheses and single quotes after `bloginfo` **A**.

5. Save and close your header.php file. Upload it to your theme directory. You will see your changes reflected on your site **B**.

To use a template tag with a query-string-style parameter:

1. Open your index.php file in a text editor or in the Edit Themes screen of your WordPress admin area.

2. Outside of the loop, add the following code to display a list of all your categories except category 3, ordered by name:

```
<ul>

<?php wp_list_categories
→ ('orderby=name&exclude=3'); ?>

</ul>
```

3. Save and close your index.php file.

continues on next page

```
<h4><?php bloginfo('description'); ?></h4>
```

A Adding a single-string PHP parameter to the `bloginfo()` tag lets you specify what you want to display.

WordPress Visual Quickstart Guide

Learn WordPress the Quick and Easy Way!

B The site's description now appears in the header, as specified by the `bloginfo()` tag.

TIP Many of the template tags that output content directly to the page in HTML format have a corresponding tag that can output the data to be manipulated with PHP functions instead. By convention, most of these are prefixed with get_, such as get_bloginfo(), which returns the same dynamic data as bloginfo() but returns the value instead of displaying it. This allows you to use PHP to manipulate the output for advanced uses.

TIP You can find a detailed listing of the available template tags on the WordPress Codex at http://codex.wordpress.org/Template_Tags.

Include Tags

Include tags are template tags that pull one WordPress template into another template. A single page in a WordPress site may be made up of several includes, such as an index page consisting of header.php, sidebar.php, and footer.php, in addition to the index.php template.

When an include tag calls for a template file that isn't part of the theme, it will use the default template in the order defined by the template hierarchy. A good example of this is a single post page (single.php) that includes a comment.php section that isn't part of the theme **C**. The effect is seamless; most viewers would have no idea that they were looking at a patchwork of templates.

To use include tags:

1. In your text editor or the Edit Themes screen in your WordPress admin area, open the template in which you would like to add an include tag.

2. Add the include tag you wish to use, such as the following:

   ```
   <div id="comments">
   <?php comments_template(); ?>
   </div>
   ```

3. Save and close your template file.

TIP More information on include tags can be found at the WordPress Codex at http://codex.wordpress.org/Include_Tags.

Evolution of WordPress

WordPress got its start way back in 2003 as a fork of the blogging platform b2, but it's come a long way since then. Major milestones include:

- The addition of plug-ins in 2004
- Theme system and static pages in 2005
- Widgets in 2007
- Shortcode API and Dashboard Widgets in 2008
- Image editing in 2009
- Custom menus and multisite management in 2010
- Post formats in 2011
- Theme customizer in 2012

By Jessica Neuman Beck July 8th, 2013
See more in: **WordPress**

Leave a Reply

Logged in as **Jessica Neuman Beck. Log out »**

[Submit Comment]

C Our theme doesn't have its own comments.php template, but WordPress provides an excellent default template that it displays as though it were part of our theme.

Conditional Tags

In addition to include tags, WordPress can use conditional tags that return Boolean **TRUE** or **FALSE** values. For example, you can use conditional tags to hide the sidebar on the home page of your site and to show it on other pages by having WordPress check to see if you're on the home page (**TRUE**) or on a different page (**FALSE**).

To use conditional tags:

1. Open your index.php file in a text editor or the Edit Themes screen in your WordPress admin area.

2. Add the following code to your file. This will display a simple message only if the current displayed page is the front page.

```php
<?php if(is_front_page())
{
echo "Welcome to the Front Page
→ of the site!";
}
?>
```

3. Save and close the index.php file.

> **TIP** You can find a detailed description of the various conditional tags and their uses at http://codex.wordpress.org/Conditional_Tags.

Using the Loop

The *loop* is the key to a WordPress theme; it is a piece of code that pulls your content from the database into your site. It's called the loop because it runs the code in a loop until all instances of the conditional HTML and PHP are satisfied. Any HTML or PHP placed inside the loop will be rendered for each post that matches the criteria within the loop tags.

The WordPress loop starts with:

```
<?php if (have_posts()); : ?>
<?php while (have_posts()) :
→ the_post(); ?>
```

and ends with

```
<?php endwhile; ?>
<?php endif; ?>
```

You can do *a lot* between those two blocks of code, but the primary thing you will need to include is the PHP function (or template tag) `<?php the_content(); ?>`. This displays the content of each of the posts that meet the criteria of the loop. Other template tags include `<?php the_title(); ?>`, which displays each post's title; `<?php the_permalink(); ?>`, which provides a link to each post's individual page; and `<?php the_category(); ?>`, which returns the categories each post has been assigned to.

Many template tags work only if they are placed inside the loop. For example, if you try to use `<?php the_content(); ?>` anywhere outside the loop in your theme, you will encounter an error.

TIP To see the loop in action and to view a full code example, check out our sample theme at www.wpvisualquickstart.com/reference/our-theme.

Putting It All Together

1. **Create a new theme folder.** Where do you upload this folder? What Is the correct way to deal with spaces in your theme's name?

2. **Add the comment that WordPress uses to identify your theme.** In which file do you add this comment? How do you differentiate comments from the rest of your CSS?

3. **Create a template file for a specific tag.** How does WordPress know which template file to use for your tag? What happens if you view another tag?

4. **Use an include tag to pull in your header.php file.** Where do you add this code?

5. **Set up the loop in your index.php template.** What does the loop do? If you add code inside the loop, how is it different from adding it outside the loop? Which tags work only when they're inside the loop?

Custom Content Types

Posts and pages are great, but if you need a greater degree of customization for your data, custom post types and taxonomies are for you.

In this chapter, we'll give you an overview of what custom post types can do and show you how to use them to set up a portfolio section for your site. We'll also walk you through the process of setting up a custom taxonomy to organize your portfolio section by feature.

Custom post types and custom taxonomies require an advanced knowledge of PHP and a familiarity with the functions.php file as well as WordPress template files.

In This Chapter

Setting Up a Custom Post Type

To use custom post types, you must first set them up in your admin area. To do this, you will add some code to your functions.php file. Then you need to create a template that will display the custom post type data on your site.

There are lots of ways to use custom post types. You can use them to set up an event database, a product catalog, or a company directory. For this example, we're creating a simple portfolio, with images and descriptions that display on a page on your site.

To set up a custom post type:

1. Using a text editor or the Edit Themes screen of your WordPress admin area, open the functions.php file.

2. Register your custom post type by adding the following code before the closing `?>` tag in your functions.php file:

```
add_action('init',
'create_portfolio');

function create_portfolio() {

$portfolio_args = array(
        'label' =>
     → __('Portfolio'),
        'singular_label' =>
     → __('Portfolio Item'),
        'public' => true,
        'show_ui' => true,
        'capability_type' =>
     → 'post',
        'hierarchical' => false,
        'rewrite' => true,
        'supports' =>
     → array('title',
     → 'editor', 'thumbnail')
```

A Once you have registered your custom post type, it will appear in your WordPress admin sidebar.

✎ **Portfolio**

Portfolio

Add New

```
);

register_post_type
→ ('portfolio',$portfolio_args);

}
```

3. Next, you need to add featured image support so that you can add images to your portfolio entries. Add the following code just below the custom post type registration:

```
add_theme_support(
→ 'post-thumbnails' );

// Custom thumbnail size

add_image_size('portfolio-thumb',
→ 300, 300, true);
```

4. Save and close the functions.php file.

5. Log in to your WordPress admin area.

   You will see a new section in your admin sidebar titled Portfolio **A**.

6. Click Add New to add your first portfolio item. The Add New Post screen will look similar to the one for adding posts and pages, but it will include only the features you specified in the custom post type registration earlier: title, editor, and thumbnail **B**.

continues on next page

The title for your portfolio item

The description for your portfolio item

Click Publish to add this portfolio item to your site

Your portfolio item's featured image

B The sections you specified in the functions.php file will appear when you add a new portfolio item.

7. Fill out the information on the Add New Post screen, and click Publish to add your portfolio item.

You will see the portfolio item in the main Portfolio list **C**.

To display a custom post type:

1. In your text editor, create a file named portfolio.php.

2. Add a comment at the top of the page to let WordPress know that this is a template:

```php
<?php
/*
Template Name: Portfolio
*/
?>
```

3. Enter the `<?php get_header(); ?>` code to pull in your header file, and add the opening `<div id="content">` tag to place the portfolio inside your content area.

4. Add the following block of code to create a custom loop that will access your portfolio posts:

```php
<?php
$loop = new WP_Query(array
→('post-type' => 'portfolio',
→'posts_per_page' => 10));
?>
<?php while ( $loop->have_posts()
→) : $loop->the_post(); ?>
```

Portfolio [Add New]

All (2) | Published (2) | Trash (2)

[Bulk Actions ▾] [Apply]   [Show all dates ▾] [Filter]

☐ Title

☐ FelineFisher

☐ WeVillage

C Your portfolio items are listed here.

Page Attributes

Parent

(no parent)

Template
Default Template
✓ Portfolio

D Choose the Portfolio template from the drop-down menu to use that template for your page.

E Your portfolio images and descriptions display on your site using your custom page template.

5. Enter the following code to display your portfolio posts:

```
<div class="portfolio-listing">
<h2><a href="<?php
→the_permalink(); ?>"><?php
→the_title(); ?></a></h2>
<?php the_post_thumbnail(
→'portfolio-thumb' ); ?>
<?php the_content(); ?>
</div>
```

6. Finally, end your custom loop, close your content tag, and call your footer:

```
<?php endwhile; ?>
</div>
<?php get_footer(); ?>
```

7. Save and close your template file, and upload it to your theme directory.

8. In your WordPress admin area, create a new page. (We called ours Our Work; you can name this page anything you want, but don't name it the exact same thing as your custom post type.) Leave the body of the page blank, but choose the Portfolio template from the drop-down menu **D**.

9. Click the Publish button on the upper-right sidebar to publish your page.

10. Navigate to your new page—in this example, Our Work—on the front end of your site. You will see your portfolio listings **E**.

TIP The example we're using is only one way to use custom post types. Get more information on the WordPress Codex at http://codex.wordpress.org/Post_Types.

Using Custom Taxonomies

Taxonomies are a way to arrange, classify, and group things. WordPress uses taxonomies in its default content types; categories and tags are both taxonomies natively supported by WordPress.

But what if you want a classification that isn't already available in the WordPress core? What if you want to be able to classify groups of products by manufacturer, events by location, or projects by type? That's where custom taxonomies come in.

To use custom taxonomies, you must first set them up by adding some code to your functions.php file. Then you need to add some code to one or more of your theme's template files to display your custom taxonomy data on your site.

For this example, you're going to expand on the portfolio custom post type you created earlier in this chapter. You'll add a taxonomy classification of Features to your portfolio listings. And you'll display those features in the custom template you created for the Our Work page.

A Once you have registered your custom taxonomy, it will appear in your admin sidebar.

B Add taxonomy terms the same way you would add tags.

To set up a custom taxonomy:

1. Using a text editor or the Edit Themes screen of your WordPress admin area, open the functions.php file.

2. Register your custom taxonomy by adding the following code after the opening **<?php** tag:

   ```
   register_taxonomy('features',
   ⟶'portfolio', array(
   ⟶'hierarchical' => false,
   ⟶'label' => 'Features',
   ⟶'query_var' => true, 'rewrite'
   ⟶=> true));
   ```

3. Save and close the functions.php file.

4. Log in to your WordPress admin area.

   You will see a new section in your admin sidebar titled Portfolio **A**.

5. Add a taxonomy term in the Add New Tag section on the Features screen **B**. You will see your new taxonomy terms appear in the list on the right **C**.

continues on next page

	Name	Description	Slug	Portfolio
☐	**Custom Content Types**		custom-content-types	0
☐	**Custom Taxonomies**		custom-taxonomies	0

C Terms you have added to your custom taxonomy are displayed in this list.

6. Click Portfolio in the sidebar menu and choose one of your portfolio items. You will see a new field called Features in the right sidebar **D**. Add the taxonomies you want to apply to that portfolio item, and click Update to save your changes. Repeat with all your other portfolio items.

> **TIP** This example is one simple way to use a custom taxonomy. To learn more about custom taxonomies and their available options, check out the WordPress Codex at http://codex.wordpress.org/Taxonomies.

D Assign taxonomy terms to your existing portfolio items. The new Features section appears when you edit each listing.

To display a custom taxonomy:

1. Open your portfolio.php file in your text editor or in the Edit Themes screen of your WordPress admin area.

2. Inside the loop that displays your custom post type, add the following code:

```php
<?php echo get_the_term_list
→($post->ID, 'features',
→'Features: ', ', ', ''); ?>
```

3. Save and close your portfolio.php file.

4. Open the Our Work page on your site. You will see your new custom taxonomy terms listed below each entry 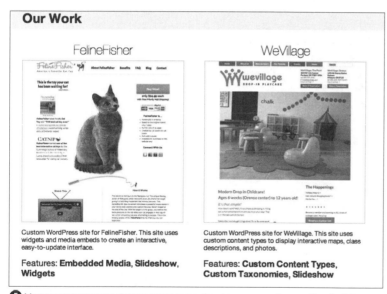.

E Your new taxonomy terms appear on the new page of your site—in this example, the Our Work page.

Putting It All Together

1. **Register a custom post type.** Where do you add this code? How do you specify additional options?

2. **Look in your WordPress admin area.** What changes after you have registered a new custom post type?

3. **Enter your custom post type items.** What options are available to you? How does this differ from the standard post or page entry screen?

4. **Create a template to display your custom post type.** How do you tell WordPress that your file is a template? What other ways might you assign a template to a custom post type?

5. **Register a custom taxonomy.** Can you apply this taxonomy to all your posts and pages, or only to your custom post type? Where do you find more information about custom taxonomies?

6. **Add a custom taxonomy display to your custom post type template.** Does this code go inside or outside of the loop? Why?

One Installation, Multiple Blogs

With WordPress MultiSite, you can run and manage an unlimited number of sites from one installation of WordPress. Each site can have its own content, users, and theme, but you need to update and maintain only one installation.

How do you do this? By creating a network! With just a few clicks, you can set up a network of sites, allow new signups, and assign privileges to your users.

The best part is that this capability is already part of your default WordPress installation—all you need to do is activate it.

Before you begin, double-check with your Web host to make sure that your hosting plan supports multiple sites. If it does, you're ready to go. Just keep in mind that running a network of sites requires a basic understanding of Unix/Linux administration as well as a solid knowledge of PHP, HTML, and CSS.

Setting Up a Network

WordPress MultiSite is part of the WordPress core, but it isn't enabled by default. To start using it, you need to set up a network.

To set up a new network:

1. Begin by backing up your existing WordPress site. You can find details on creating WordPress backups in Chapter 16, "Best Practices."

What Is WordPress MultiSite?

WordPress MultiSite began as a separate project known as WordPress MU (or Multi User). In the 3.0 WordPress update, the WordPress MU code was merged with the WordPress core to give all users the ability to create a network of Web sites from one WordPress installation.

A standard WordPress installation gives you one site (for example, www.wpvisualquickstart.com). Using WordPress MultiSite, you can allow users to set up their own subsites (subsite.wpvisualquickstart.com if you are using subdomains, for example, or wpvisualquickstart.com/subsite if you are using subdirectories).

To get a better idea of WordPress MultiSite in action, look no further than WordPress.com Ⓐ. It uses MultiSite to run a network of around *20 million* blogs.

Ⓐ WordPress.com is a great example of a MultiSite installation running many different subsites.

```
/**
 * For developers: WordPress debugging mode.
 *
 * Change this to true to enable the display of notices during development.
 * It is strongly recommended that plugin and theme developers use WP_DEBUG
 * in their development environments.
 */
define('WP_DEBUG', false);

define('WP_ALLOW_MULTISITE', true);
/* That's all, stop editing! Happy blogging. */

/** Absolute path to the WordPress directory. */
if ( !defined('ABSPATH') )
    define('ABSPATH', dirname(__FILE__) . '/');

/** Sets up WordPress vars and included files. */
require_once(ABSPATH . 'wp-settings.php');
```

B Add the code to enable MultiSite to your wp-config.php file.

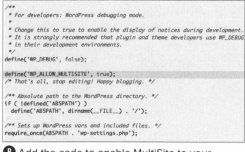

C You will see a Network Setup option under Tools in the admin sidebar menu.

Create a Network of WordPress Sites

Welcome to the Network installation process!

Fill in the information below and you'll be on your way to creating a network of WordPress sites. We will create configuration files in the next step.

Note: Please make sure the Apache mod_rewrite module is installed as it will be used at the end of this installation.

If mod_rewrite is disabled, ask your administrator to enable that module, or look at the Apache documentation or elsewhere for help setting it up.

Addresses of Sites in your Network

Please choose whether you would like sites in your WordPress network to use sub-domains or sub-directories. **You cannot change this later.**

You will need a wildcard DNS record if you are going to use the virtual host (sub-domain) functionality.

○ Sub-domains   like site1.multi.wpvisualquickstart.com and site2.multi.wpvisualquickstart.com
◉ Sub-directories   like multi.wpvisualquickstart.com/site1 and multi.wpvisualquickstart.com/site2

Network Details

Server Address   The internet address of your network will be multi.wpvisualquickstart.com.

Network Title   WordPress Visual Quickstart Guide Sites
                     What would you like to call your network?

Admin E-mail Address info@couldbestudios.com
                     Your email address.

[Install]

D Double-check your options before clicking Install.

2. Choose the URL structure for your subsites. If you want to use subdirectories (yoursite.com/subsite), great! You can go on to the next step. If you want to use subdomains (subsite.yourdomain.com), see the "Setting Up Wildcard Subdomains" sidebar.

3. Using an FTP client, navigate to your wp-config.php file in your main WordPress directory. Open the wp-config file in a text editor, and add this line of code above the line that says /* **That's all, stop editing! Happy blogging.** */ **B**:

    ```
    define('WP_ALLOW_MULTISITE',
    →true);
    ```

    Save and close your wp-config.php file.

4. In your WordPress admin area, click the Tools sidebar menu. You will see a new menu item, Network Setup **C**.

5. Click Network Setup to open the Create A Network Of WordPress Sites screen **D**. If you have set up wildcard subdomains, you can choose to enable them here. Fields such as Network Title and Admin E-mail Address will be prepopulated using the data you provided earlier in the General Settings screen; double-check that the information is correct, and then click Install.

continues on next page

6. Next, you need to enable the network by adding some special code to your wp-config.php file and your .htaccess file **Ⓔ**. You will see a message at the top of this screen recommending that you back up your existing wp-config.php and .htaccess files **Ⓕ**.

7. Open the wp-config file in a text editor, and add this block of code above the line that says **/* That's all, stop editing! Happy blogging. */**:

```
define( 'MULTISITE', true );

define( 'SUBDOMAIN_INSTALL',
→true );

$base = '/';

define( 'DOMAIN_CURRENT_SITE',
→'demo.wpvisualquickstart.com' );

define( 'PATH_CURRENT_SITE', '/' );

define( 'SITE_ID_CURRENT_SITE',
→1 );

define( 'BLOG_ID_CURRENT_SITE',
→1 );
```

Save and close your wp-config.php file.

1. Add the following to your `wp-config.php` file in `/home/wordpres/public_html/multi/` **above** the line reading `/* That's all, stop editing! Happy blogging. */` :

```
define('MULTISITE', true);
define('SUBDOMAIN_INSTALL', false);
define('DOMAIN_CURRENT_SITE', 'multi.wpvisualquickstart.com');
define('PATH_CURRENT_SITE', '/');
define('SITE_ID_CURRENT_SITE', 1);
define('BLOG_ID_CURRENT_SITE', 1);
```

2. Add the following to your `.htaccess` file in `/home/wordpres/public_html/multi/` , replacing other WordPress rules:

```
RewriteEngine On
RewriteBase /
RewriteRule ^index\.php$ - [L]

# add a trailing slash to /wp-admin
RewriteRule ^([_0-9a-zA-Z-]+/)?wp-admin$ $1wp-admin/ [R=301,L]

RewriteCond %{REQUEST_FILENAME} -f [OR]
RewriteCond %{REQUEST_FILENAME} -d
RewriteRule ^ - [L]
RewriteRule ^([_0-9a-zA-Z-]+/)?(wp-(content|admin|includes).*) $2 [L]
RewriteRule ^([_0-9a-zA-Z-]+/)?(.*\.php)$ $2 [L]
RewriteRule . index.php [L]
```

Ⓔ Follow the instructions on this page to add blocks of code to your wp-config.php file and your .htaccess file.

Caution: We recommend you back up your existing `wp-config.php` and `.htaccess` files.

Ⓕ Back up your files before making changes.

G You may need to show invisible files before you can make changes to your .htaccess file.

H Click the Log In link to log back in to your admin area.

I When MultiSite is enabled, you will see a My Sites link in your admin top bar.

8. Open your .htaccess file in a text editor. If you do not see your .htaccess file in the list of files in your root directory, you may need to tell your FTP client to show invisible files **G**.

Replace any code in your .htaccess file with the following:

```
RewriteEngine On
RewriteBase /
RewriteRule ^index\.php$ - [L]


# uploaded files
RewriteRule ^files/(.+)
wp-includes/ms-files.php?file=
$1 [L]


RewriteCond %{REQUEST_FILENAME}
-f [OR]
RewriteCond %{REQUEST_FILENAME}
-d
RewriteRule ^ - [L]
RewriteRule . index.php [L]
```

Save and close your .htaccess file.

9. Click the link at the bottom of the Create A Network Of WordPress Sites page to log in to your admin area again **H**.

You will now see a link to My Sites in your Dashboard sidebar menu as well as a new My Sites link in the admin bar **I**.

Your WordPress installation is now configured for MultiSite.

To update an existing WordPress MU installation:

1. Begin by backing up your existing WordPress site. You can find details on creating WordPress backups in Chapter 2, "Get Familiar with WordPress."

2. Upgrade your WordPress installation to the latest version. (Refer to Chapter 2 for an explanation of the upgrade process.)

3. When your upgrade is complete, you will see a warning message letting you know that you will need to make a change to your wp-config.php file. The message will include a line of code that defines **NONCE_SALT**, along with a string of numbers, letters, and symbols that is unique to your installation. Copy that line of code, and add it to your wp-config.php file just above the line that says **/* That's all, stop editing! Happy blogging. */**.

   Save and close your wp-config file.

4. Open your .htaccess file in a text editor. If you do not see your .htaccess file in the list of files in your root directory, you may need to tell your FTP client to show invisible files. Replace the RewriteRule that reads **RewriteRule ^(.*/)?files/ (.*) wp-includes/blogs.php?file=$2 [L]** with the following:

   ```
   RewriteRule ^(.*/)?files/(.*)
   → wp-includes/ms-files.php?file=
   → $2 [L]
   ```

   Save and close your .htaccess file.

5. Navigate to your wp-content folder, and delete the blogs.php file.

   Your WordPress MU installation has now been upgraded to WordPress MultiSite.

Setting Up Wildcard Subdomains

A wildcard in Web hosting is represented with an asterisk (*). The * represents a nonexistent domain name; in this case, it's a placeholder for your subdomain names that have not yet been generated.

If you want the URLs for your new subsites to display as subdomains, you will need to do two things:

- Configure Apache to accept wildcards
- Add a wildcard subdomain to the DNS records on your server

Here's an example of how to do this using cPanel:

1. Open the httpd.conf file or the include file containing the VHOST entry for your Web account.

2. Add this line:

   ```
   ServerAlias *.example.com
   ```

3. Log in to your cPanel. Create a subdomain called * (*.example.com). Make sure the subdomain is pointed to the same folder where your wp-config.php file is located.

Because every Web host is configured differently, we strongly recommend contacting your hosting company for specific directions on setting up wildcard subdomains.

J You can switch between Network Admin and Site Admin by using the drop-down menu under My Sites.

To add a new networked blog:

1. Hover over the My Sites link in the top bar. In the Network Admin submenu, click Sites **J**.

2. On the Sites screen, click Add New **K**.

3. Add your information to the Site Address, Site Title, and Admin Email fields **L**. Click Add Site.

   Your new site has been created.

> **TIP** You can allow users to create their own subsites by enabling front-end signups. Log in to your Network Admin Dashboard, and click Settings. Under Allow New Registrations, choose Both Sites And User Accounts Can Be Registered, and click Save Changes. Your users will now be able to sign up for new sites at yourdomain.com/wp-signup.php.

K Click Add New to create a new site on your network.

L Fill out the information, and click Add Site.

Administrating a Blog Network

Once your network is set up, you'll need to make changes to your settings to get everything working the way you want it to.

In your Network Admin area, click Settings in the sidebar menu to open the settings for your network **A**. Set your Operational Settings here as well as your Registration Settings. You can set banned names (names that you do not want people to use for subsites), limit registrations to specific domains, and ban certain email domain names here as well **B**.

You can also set defaults for your New Site Settings, including the text that will display for email confirmations and default posts and pages on new sites **C**.

A Click Network Admin and then Settings to see the settings for your network.

B Choose what to ban and what to allow by entering domain names or keywords into these fields.

C Choose what displays on new sites in your network in New Site Settings.

Upload Settings		
Site upload space	☐ Limit total size of files uploaded to 100 ⊟ MB	
Upload file types	jpg jpeg png gif mp3 mov avi wmv midi mid pdf	
Max upload file size	1500 ⊟ KB	
Menu Settings		
Enable administration menus	☐ Plugins	

D Decide what your users can upload to their networked sites here. Be sure to click Save Changes when you're done!

E Manage users on your network by clicking Users in your Network Admin area.

F All users on your network are listed here. The Super Admin is a user with access to the Network Admin area.

G When editing a user in the Network Admin area, you can choose to assign or revoke Super Admin status.

Set your Upload Settings to allow or restrict different file type uploads for your subsite users. You can also choose to give your users access to administrative menus, such as the one that gives them the ability to install plug-ins on their subsites **D**.

TIP You can always switch back and forth between Network and Site admin modes by clicking the My Sites drop-down menu at the top left of any admin page.

To manage users on a network:

1. In your Network Admin area, click Users in the sidebar menu **E**.

2. You will see a list of users along with the date each one registered and the sites on your network that they are a part of **F**. You will also see a listing for Super Admin; users with this designation are the only ones able to access the Network Admin area to make changes to the network.

3. To make changes to a user, click the user's name and modify information on the Edit User screen **G**. You can also assign Super Admin privileges here. Remember, anyone with Super Admin status has access to your entire network, so use caution!

continues on next page

To delete a user, hover over the user's name in the main Users list and click the Delete button **H**. You will be prompted to transfer or delete the user's posts and links before you confirm deletion **I**.

To add plug-ins to a network:

1. In your Network Admin area, click Plugins in the left sidebar menu **J**.

2. Click Add New to add a new plug-in **K**.

3. Once your plug-in is installed, click Network Activate **L**.

TIP Only a Super Admin can add plug-ins to a network.

To set a new default theme for networked blogs:

1. In your Network Admin area, click Themes, and then click Installed Themes.

2. Find the theme you want to assign as the default in your list of available themes. If it is not already network enabled, click the Network Enable link below the theme's name **M**.

H Hover over a user's name to see the Delete option.

I You can delete a user's posts and links or assign them to another user before confirming deletion of the user.

J You see your available plug-ins in the Network Admin area by clicking the Plugins menu in the sidebar.

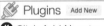

K Click Add New to add a new plug-in.

L Click Network Activate to make your new plug-in available to all sites on your network.

M Be sure the theme you want to assign as the new default has been enabled across your network. Choose Network Enable below your theme name to enable a theme to all your subsites.

```
define( 'PATH_CURRENT_SITE', '/' );
define( 'SITE_ID_CURRENT_SITE', 1 );
define( 'BLOG_ID_CURRENT_SITE', 1 );
define('WP_DEFAULT_THEME', 'our-theme');

/* That's all, stop editing! Happy blogging. */
```

Ⓝ Add the code to your wp-config.php file to assign a new default theme to your networked sites.

3. Using an FTP client, navigate to your wp-config.php file in your main WordPress directory. Open the wp-config file in a text editor and add this line of code above the line that says **/* That's all, stop editing! Happy blogging. */**:

> define('WP_DEFAULT_THEME',
> → 'our-theme');

(Replace the words **our-theme** with the name of any installed theme you would like to use as the default for new sites on your network **Ⓝ**.)

4. Save and close your wp-config.php file.

New subsite users will now see the theme you have chosen as the default theme for their site.

TIP Clicking **Network Disable** next to any installed theme will remove it from the list of themes your users can choose from.

Putting It All Together

1. **Set up WordPress MultiSite.** What files do you need to modify in order to activate MultiSite?

2. **Modify the settings for your network.** Where do you access these settings? Do your users have access to these settings?

3. **Create a subsite.** What happens if you try to use a name that is on your banned list?

4. **Assign a new default theme.** Can you assign a default theme that has not been network enabled? How do you network-enable a theme?

More Ways to
Customize WordPress

You've got the theme—now add some flair! In this chapter, we'll show you some of the many ways you can customize WordPress. For example, you'll learn how to activate and use Jetpack, a popular plug-in that adds such features as built-in social networking, enhanced commenting, forms, and more. We'll also teach you how to integrate Google Ads to monetize your site and how to set up Google Web Fonts to give your text some flair. Finally, we'll walk you through the process of setting up and displaying your RSS feed, so your fans never miss a post.

Setting Up and Using Jetpack

Self-hosted WordPress users can now take advantage of the coolest features of WordPress.com. Jetpack is a plug-in suite developed by Automattic that lets you selectively activate such add-ons as social networking, enhanced commenting, custom forms, slideshows, and more. You can activate and manage each add-on separately, and new ones are being added all the time.

Jetpack is cloud-based, so to use it, you'll need to connect your site with a free WordPress.com account.

To set up Jetpack:

1. Go to Plugins > Add New, search for Jetpack, and click Install Now.

2. After the plug-in installs, click the Activate Now link to activate it. You will see a message at the top of your screen telling you to connect your site to WordPress.com **A**. Click the green Connect To WordPress.com button to continue.

3. Enter your WordPress.com account login information (or click the Need An Account link to set up a new WordPress.com account), and click Authorize Jetpack **B**.

    You will be redirected back to your site and see a "Connected to WordPress. com" notification at the top right of your screen, as well as a "Welcome to Jetpack" message **C**.

A Click the Connect to WordPress.com button to finish activating your Jetpack plug-in.

B Enter your WordPress.com login credentials, and click the Authorize Jetpack button.

C When you have connected to a valid WordPress.com account, you will be redirected back to the Jetpack screen in your admin area.

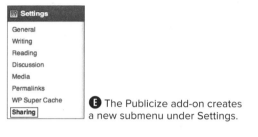

D Select a Jetpack add-on, and click the Configure button to get started.

E The Publicize add-on creates a new submenu under Settings.

F Click the Add A New Connection links to be able to notify your favorite social networks each time you make a new post.

To use a Jetpack add-on:

1. Click the Jetpack link in the admin sidebar to open the main Jetpack screen. Choose the add-on you'd like to use, and click the Configure button on the lower right **D**.

   In this example, we're configuring the Publicize add-on. This add-on creates a new link in the Settings submenu called Sharing **E**.

2. To automatically share new blog posts when they're published, find the social networking site you'd like to enable and click the Add New Connection link for that site **F**. Authorize the application in your social network of choice by following the instructions in the pop-up that appears. Repeat for each social network you'd like to enable.

3. Below the automatic sharing section, you will see a block of Sharing Buttons **G**. Drag buttons from Available Services to Enabled Services to display them on your site.

   continues on next page

Sharing Buttons

Add sharing buttons to your blog and allow your visitors to share posts with their friends.

Available Services

Drag and drop the services you'd like to enable into the box below.

Add a new service

Print   Tumblr   Pinterest

Enabled Services

Services dragged here will appear individually.

Email   Twitter   Facebook   LinkedIn   Pocket
Digg   Reddit   StumbleUpon   Google +1

Services dragged here will be hidden behind a share button.

Live Preview   Share this:

G Choose the sharing buttons you'd like to display on your site by dragging them from Available Services to Enabled Services.

4. Choose the button style and the sharing label, and choose whether to open links in a new window. You can also choose which sections of your site will display the sharing buttons **H**.

5. Save your changes. Your sharing settings are updated.

H Configure your sharing options here.

To activate a new Jetpack add-on:

1. Click the Jetpack link in the admin sidebar to open the main Jetpack screen, and find the yet-to-be activated add-on you'd like to use. Add-ons that have not been activated are grayed-out and display a blue Activate button at the lower left **I**. Click the Activate button to activate the add-on.

2. Click the Configure button (lower right) to configure your add-on **J**. In this example, we've activated the Likes add-on, which adds an extra section to the Publicize settings.

3. Find the new section on the Publicize screen (it will be highlighted yellow the first time you visit), and choose whether to display WordPress Likes on all your posts or to activate it on a post-by-post basis **K**.

4. Save your changes.

> **TIP** Jetpack itself is a free plug-in, and most of the add-ons are free. Be aware, however, that a few (like VaultPress and Akismet) are paid additions. Be sure to click the More Information button on each add-on to check its status if you have any questions.

I Click the Activate button to activate a new Jetpack add-on.

J Activated add-on modules display a Configure button. Click it to configure the add-on.

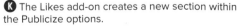

K The Likes add-on creates a new section within the Publicize options.

A Find the ad unit you want to display on your site, and click the Get Code link.

B Copy the code generated by Google to add it to your site.

C Paste the ad code into a text widget.

D Your Google ad will now display on your site.

Monetizing Your Site: Ad Integration

Ads are a good way to make money from your Web site, and Google AdSense is one of the largest services providing online advertising. This section will walk you through the process of adding Google AdSense code to your site's sidebar.

You'll need an active Google AdSense account with at least one ad unit set up. You can sign up for Google AdSense or access your existing account at google.com/adsense.

To use Google AdSense:

1. Log in to your Google AdSense account, and click My Ads to see your available ads.

2. Choose the ad unit you want to display on your site, and click Get Code **A**.

3. Copy the ad code (Ctrl+C on Windows, Command+C on a Mac) **B**.

4. In your WordPress admin area, go to Appearance > Widgets. Drag a text widget into your sidebar, and paste the Google AdSense code you selected in step 3 into the body of the text widget **C**.

5 Click Save to save your changes. Google ads will now display in your sidebar **D**.

Using Google Fonts

Want to take your text beyond Times New Roman and Arial? Web fonts are fonts that have been specially licensed for use on the Web. With a snippet of code, you can transform your text into something with a bit more personality.

You can add Web font support to your site in a few different ways. In this section, we will walk you through setting up Web fonts using one of the easiest (and free) Web font providers: Google Fonts.

To use Google Fonts:

1. Go to google.com/fonts to browse the available fonts **A**.

2. Select the font you'd like to use on your site, and click the Quick Use icon **B**.

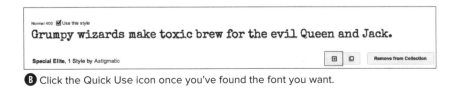

A Browse through Google's free collection of Web fonts to find the one you want for your site.

B Click the Quick Use icon once you've found the font you want.

3. In the detail screen for your selected font, scroll down until you see the code to add to your site. Copy the code (Ctrl+C on Windows, Command+C on a Mac) **C**.

4. In the admin area of your site, go to Appearance > Editor and open the header.php file. Paste the code you copied in step 4 into the **<head>** area of the file **D**. Save the header.php file.

5. Open the style.css file. Find the section of your site you want to style with your chosen Web font. Add the name of the font after the words **font-family** to change the font on your site **E**. Save your style.css file.

6. View your site to see your new font in action **F**.

```
Standard   @import   Javascript

3. Add this code to your website:

<link href='http://fonts.googleapis.com/css?family=Special+Elite' rel='stylesheet' type='text/css'>
```

C Copy the code to add to your site.

```
<!DOCTYPE html PUBLIC "-//W3C//DTD XHTML 1.0 Transitional//EN" "http://www.w3.org/TR/xhtml1/DTD/xhtml1-
transitional.dtd">
<html <?php language_attributes(); ?> xmlns:fb="https://www.facebook.com/2008/fbml" xmlns:og="http://ogp.me/ns#">
<head>
        <meta charset="<?php bloginfo( 'charset' ); ?>" />
        <title>
                <?php bloginfo('name'); ?> <?php wp_title(); ?>
        </title>
        <link rel="profile" href="http://gmpg.org/xfn/11" />
        <link rel="stylesheet" type="text/css" media="all" href="<?php bloginfo( 'stylesheet_url' ); ?>" />
        <link rel="shortcut icon" href="<?php bloginfo('stylesheet_directory'); ?>/favicon.ico" />
        <link rel="pingback" href="<?php bloginfo( 'pingback_url' ); ?>" />
        <link href='http://fonts.googleapis.com/css?family=Special+Elite' rel='stylesheet' type='text/css'>
<?php wp_head(); ?>
```

D Paste the Google Web Font code into your header.php file.

```
.entry h2 a {
font-family: 'Special Elite', cursive;
}
```
E Add the Web font to the selector you'd like to affect in your style.css file.

Evolution of WordPress

WordPress got its start way back in 2003 as a fork of the blogging platform b2, but it's come a long way since then. Major milestones include:

- The addition of plug-ins in 2004
- Theme system and static pages in 2005
- Widgets in 2007

F Your new Web font now appears on your site.

RSS Feeds

One of the most popular ways to allow people to follow your posts is to syndicate the posts in an RSS feed. WordPress automatically creates an RSS feed for your posts, so all you need to do is configure it to your liking.

In this section, we'll show you how to set up subscriptions to your posts and comments, as well as how to display a link to your feed on your site so subscribers have an easy way of adding you to their reading lists.

To configure your RSS feed:

1. Choose Settings > Reading in the left sidebar menu to access the feed settings.

2. On the Reading Settings page, find the section dealing with syndication **A**. For the "Syndication feeds show the most recent items" field, choose the maximum number of posts that will appear in your feed at one time (for example, when a new subscriber adds your feed). The default is 10.

3. Below the syndication option, you will see choices for displaying individual articles in your feed. Choose either Full Text or Summary.

   If you choose Full Text, entire blog posts will be shown when people read your feed. If you choose Summary, WordPress will display either the excerpt of your posts or the *teaser*, which consists of the first 55 words of each of your posts.

4. Click Save Changes.

A Choose the number and format for your RSS feeds.

B Drag the Meta widget into your sidebar to display your feeds and other useful links.

C The Meta widget on a sidebar.

D An RSS widget displaying the feed for an external site.

To display links to your feeds:

1. Choose Appearance > Widgets in the left sidebar menu.

2. Find the Meta widget, and drag it to your widgetized sidebar area. (If you're unsure how to use widgets, check out Chapter 6, "Widgets and Plug-ins.")

3. Once in a widgetized sidebar area, the widget will expand to reveal the available options. For the Meta widget, the available configuration option is the title **B**. Enter the title you'd like to use for your Meta widget, and click Save at the bottom of the widget.

4. Check your site: Your sidebar now includes a section with links to your feeds as well as other useful links **C**.

TIP Most browsers will display a button or an icon next to the URL for a page with a valid RSS feed. Clicking the button or icon will open the feed in your RSS reader of choice.

Advanced Uses for RSS

RSS can be used for all sorts of things. Check out these tips for some advanced ways you can use your RSS feed.

- You can use the RSS widget to add external feeds (or even your own feeds) to your site **D**. You can combine your external feeds with the Recent Posts or Recent Comments widget to add a second list of feeds with alternate styling.

- You can incorporate your Flickr photos or Twitter posts with your blog feed, updating your readers each time you add to those services.

- Using WordPress categories, you can create a feed specific to certain interests, such as podcasting. That way, readers can subscribe only to the posts they want to see.

Putting It All Together

1. **Activate the Jetpack plug-in.** What add-ons are available to you? How do you configure an add-on?

2. **Add Google AdSense to your sidebar.** Where do you paste the code?

3. **Use a Web font in your site's header.** What files do you need to modify in order to add the Google Fonts code?

4. **Display a link to your RSS feed.** What other methods can you use to access your RSS feed?

16

Best Practices

A great-looking site is the perfect basis for a successful online presence, but to get the most out of your WordPress installation, you'll need a few tricks up your sleeve. This section will teach you about the basics of search engine optimization (SEO) and show how to speed up WordPress by making informed plug-in choices and by using site caching. Finally, we'll show you how to back up your data so you never lose a thing.

In This Chapter

Search Engine Optimization

One modification people are often eager to make is the addition of search engine optimization (SEO) features. SEO makes your site more visible to search engines, allowing you to rank higher in search results.

One way to optimize your site is to add search engine-friendly keywords and descriptions. Several WordPress plug-ins are available that make this process easy. This section will walk you through setup and configuration of the popular WordPress SEO plug-in called All In One SEO Pack.

A Click All In One SEO in the sidebar to access the configuration options.

To use All In One SEO Pack:

1. In your WordPress admin sidebar, click Plugins > Add New and add the All In One SEO Pack plug-in. For instructions on how to add a plug-in, see Chapter 6, "Widgets and Plug-ins."

2. Activate the All In One SEO Pack plug-in.

3. Find the All In One SEO link in your admin sidebar **A**. Click General Settings to configure the plug-in.

4. Enter your Home Page Settings **B**. This meta information is displayed to search engines indexing your site.

B Enter Home Page Settings to provide general information about your site to Google and other search engines.

Keyword Settings

(?)	Use Keywords:	⊙ Enabled	○ Disabled
(?)	Use Categories for META keywords:	☐	
(?)	Use Tags for META keywords:	☑	
(?)	Dynamically Generate Keywords for Posts Page:	☑	

C Enabling keywords allows the All In One SEO plug-in to dynamically generate keywords that are search-engine friendly for your content.

Title Settings

(?)	Rewrite Titles:	⊙ Enabled	○ Disabled
(?)	Capitalize Titles:	☑	
(?)	Capitalize Category Titles:	☑	
(?)	Page Title Format:	%page_title% I %blog_title%	
(?)	Post Title Format:	%post_title% I %blog_title%	

D The Rewrite Titles option gives you control over the way your titles display in browsers and search engine results.

5. Enter your Keyword Settings **C**. You can choose to use categories and tags to create keywords for search engines, and you can choose to dynamically generate keywords based on your posts.

6. Choose your Title Settings. If you enable the Rewrite Titles option **D**, your page titles (which display at the top of your browser and also in search engine results) will be rewritten to the formats you specify in this section.

7. Select whether you want to use SEO for your custom post types, and toggle the Display Settings to show or hide SEO options on the edit screen for posts and pages.

8. Continue to scroll through the options to add integration with various Webmaster Tools services and Google-specific services, as well as advanced settings. All of these fields are optional, so if you don't know what they mean, just leave them blank.

   When you're happy with your choices, click Update Options at the bottom of the screen to save your configuration.

continues on next page

9. Navigate to an existing post or page and click Edit. Near the bottom of the screen you will see a section for All In One SEO Pack. Enter a title specific to that page (in this example, the title is specific to the About page) and a description of the page's content **E**. Try to keep the description under 160 characters. When you're done, click Update to update your page.

Your new search engine-friendly title and description will now appear in search results.

TIP Click the question mark icon next to any option on the All In One SEO general settings screen to learn more.

TIP It may take up to a day or two for search engine results to display your updated information, so don't panic if your changes aren't reflected right away.

TIP Tailor your descriptions of each page or post; this description will show up in targeted search results.

TIP Learn more about SEO for WordPress on the WordPress Codex: http://codex.wordpress.org/Search_Engine_Optimization_for_WordPress.

All in One SEO Pack

Upgrade to All in One SEO Pack Pro Version

(?) **Preview Snippet**

About Jessica Neuman Beck and Matt Beck | WordPress Visual Quickstart...
http://www.wpvisualquickstart.com/about/
Learn about Jessica Neuman Beck and Matt Beck, authors of the WordPress Visual QuickStart Guide from Peachpit Press.

(?) **Title**

About Jessica Neuman Beck and Matt Beck

39 | characters. Most search engines use a maximum of 60 chars for the title.

(?) **Description**

Learn about Jessica Neuman Beck and Matt Beck, authors of the WordPress Visual QuickStart Guide from Peachpit Press.

116 | characters. Most search engines use a maximum of 160 chars for the description.

E The information you enter into the All In One SEO Pack section appears when you link to a page or post as well as in search engine results.

Keep It Clean: Coding Advice

When a search engine indexes your Web site, it isn't seeing your snazzy layout or your beautiful graphics; it's viewing your raw code **F**. That's one reason it's important to follow common coding guidelines—to make it as easy as possible for search engines to know what your site is all about.

Here are some tips to help make your code search-engine friendly:

- Make sure your theme uses clearly defined headers (**\<h1\>**, **\<h2\>**, **\<h3\>**, etc.) to denote hierarchy.

- Always use alternative text for your images. When you add an image in the WordPress Media Library, you will see an option to add alternative text **G**; this is the text that the search engine sees in place of your image, so it should briefly describe what your image is about.

- Don't paste text directly from a word processing program like Microsoft Word. Programs like this often surround text in markup that not only can affect your site's layout but can also negatively affect your search engine readability. If you are pasting from a word processing program into WordPress, click the Kitchen Sink button in your Visual Editor, and then click the Paste From Word button **H**. You can paste your text into the modal window that appears **I**, and WordPress will strip out the errant markup before adding the text to your post.

```
<!DOCTYPE html PUBLIC "-//W3C//DTD XHTML 1.0 Transitional//EN" "http://www.w3.org/TR/xhtml1/DTD/xhtml1-transitional.dtd">
<html lang="en-US" xmlns:fb="https://www.facebook.com/2008/fbml" xmlns:og="http://ogp.me/ns#">
<head>
        <meta charset="UTF-8" />
        <title>Evolution of WordPress | WordPress Visual Quickstart Guide</title>
        <link rel="profile" href="http://gmpg.org/xfn/11" />
        <link rel="stylesheet" type="text/css" media="all" href="http://www.wpvisualquickstart.com/wp-content/themes/our-theme/style.css" />
        <link rel="shortcut icon" href="http://www.wpvisualquickstart.com/wp-content/themes/our-theme/favicon.ico" />
        <link rel="pingback" href="http://www.wpvisualquickstart.com/xmlrpc.php" />
        <link href='http://fonts.googleapis.com/css?family=Special+Elite' rel='stylesheet' type='text/css'>
<link rel="alternate" type="application/rss+xml" title="WordPress Visual Quickstart Guide &raquo; Evolution of WordPress Comments Feed"
 href="http://www.wpvisualquickstart.com/2013/evolution-of-wordpress/feed/" />
<link rel='stylesheet' id='jetpack_likes-css'  href='http://www.wpvisualquickstart.com/wp-content/plugins/jetpack/modules/likes/style.css?
ver=2.3.5' type='text/css' media='all' />
<link rel='stylesheet' id='admin-bar-css'  href='http://www.wpvisualquickstart.com/wp-includes/css/admin-bar.min.css' type='text/css'
 media='all' />
<link rel='stylesheet' id='easy-fancybox-css-css'  href='http://www.wpvisualquickstart.com/wp-content/plugins/easy-fancybox/easy-
fancybox.css.php?ver=1.3.5' type='text/css' media='screen' />
<link rel='stylesheet' id='jetpack-widgets-css'  href='http://www.wpvisualquickstart.com/wp-
content/plugins/jetpack/modules/widgets/widgets.css?ver=20121003' type='text/css' media='all' />
<link rel='stylesheet' id='sharedaddy-css'  href='http://www.wpvisualquickstart.com/wp-
content/plugins/jetpack/modules/sharedaddy/sharing.css?ver=2.3.5' type='text/css' media='all' />
<script type='text/javascript' src='http://www.wpvisualquickstart.com/wp-includes/js/jquery/jquery.js?ver=1.10.2'></script>
<script type='text/javascript' src='http://www.wpvisualquickstart.com/wp-includes/js/jquery/jquery-migrate.min.js?ver=1.2.1'></script>
<script type='text/javascript' src='http://www.wpvisualquickstart.com/wp-content/plugins/jetpack/_inc/postmessage.js?ver=2.3.5'></script>
<script type='text/javascript' src='http://www.wpvisualquickstart.com/wp-content/plugins/jetpack/_inc/jquery.inview.js?ver=2.3.5'></script>
<script type='text/javascript' src='http://www.wpvisualquickstart.com/wp-content/plugins/jetpack/_inc/jquery.jetpack-resize.js?ver=2.3.5'>
</script>
<link rel="EditURI" type="application/rsd+xml" title="RSD" href="http://www.wpvisualquickstart.com/xmlrpc.php?rsd" />
<link rel="wlwmanifest" type="application/wlwmanifest+xml" href="http://www.wpvisualquickstart.com/wp-includes/wlwmanifest.xml" />
<link rel='prev' title='Tutorial: Using the Theme Customizer' href='http://www.wpvisualquickstart.com/2012/tutorial-using-the-theme-
customizer/' />
<meta name="generator" content="WordPress 3.7-alpha-25000" />
<link rel='canonical' href='http://www.wpvisualquickstart.com/2013/evolution-of-wordpress/' />
<link rel='shortlink' href='http://wp.me/p1AnJQ-9n' />

<!-- Jetpack Open Graph Tags -->
<meta property="og:type" content="article" />
```

F What a search engine "sees" when crawling your site.

Caption

Alternative Text

Description

| b | i | link | b-quote | del | ins | img | ul | ol | li | code | close tags |

G Add alternative text to describe images to search engines.

Paste from Word

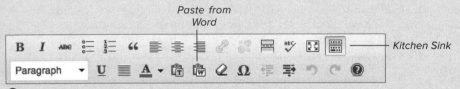

Kitchen Sink

H Click the Kitchen Sink button to reveal additional formatting options, and then click the Paste From Word button to open the Paste From Word overlay.

Paste from Word   ✕

Paste from Word
Use CTRL + V on your keyboard to paste the text into the window.

I Paste text you have copied from a Word document into this box. WordPress will remove any extraneous markup before adding it to your post.

Cancel   Insert

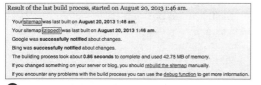

A Click the Click Here link to generate your first sitemap.

B Information about your most recently generated sitemap displays here. Click the links to view your sitemap or download a ZIP file for your records.

Setting Up a Sitemap

A properly generated XML sitemap can make a huge difference in how effectively a search engine can crawl your content. A sitemap lists all the posts and pages on your site and lets search engines know which have been updated recently. A good sitemap will ensure that all of your content is indexed correctly.

In this section, we will walk you through the process of setting up a sitemap using the Google XML Sitemaps plug-in.

To set up a sitemap:

1. In your WordPress admin sidebar, click Plugins > Add New, and install the Google XML Sitemaps plug-in. When the plug-in has installed, click Activate Plugin to activate it.

2. Go to Settings > XML-Sitemap to set up your first sitemap. You will see a message at the top of the screen letting you know that no sitemap has been generated for your site **A**. Click the Click Here link to build your first sitemap.

3. When your sitemap has been generated, you will see an overview of the sitemap's details **B**. You can view your sitemap by clicking the sitemap link, or download a ZIP file for your records by clicking the zipped link.

> **TIP** You can tweak the type of sitemap generated, the building mode, update notifications, and more for your sitemap by editing the configuration sections below the build results.

Speeding Up Your Site

The speed with which your site loads can be the difference between a popular site and an abandoned one. As a general rule, people don't like to wait a long time for a site to appear on their screens, so the faster your site loads, the better.

To that end, many sites utilize *caching*. Caching serves up a static version of your dynamic files rather than processing your site's PHP scripts each time a page loads. Caching programs can be configured to refresh the static page after a certain amount of time so that the content is always fresh.

In this section, you'll learn how to set up WP Super Cache, a popular WordPress plug-in that gives you tons of configuration options.

Choose Plug-ins Wisely

Plug-ins are a great way to make your site work exactly the way you want it to—but too much of a good thing can be detrimental to your site's performance. Each plug-in performs a small function; if you're requiring your site to load lots of these functions each time someone views a page, your site may experience slowness.

To help prevent this, regularly check your plug-ins to make sure you aren't loading things you don't use anymore. Be sure that when you install new plug-ins you aren't duplicating the functionality of an existing plug-in (for example, adding several different stats plug-ins to check stats from various sources). It's also a good idea to ask yourself if you really need each new plug-in you install; adding lots of widgets to your sidebar, for example, might not add anything useful to your site—but they might slow it down.

To set up WP Super Cache:

1. In your WordPress admin sidebar, click Plugins > Add New, and add the WP Super Cache plug-in. For instructions on how to add a plug-in, see Chapter 6, "Widgets and Plug-ins."

2. Activate the WP Super Cache plug-in. You will see a notice at the top of your screen alerting you that the WP Super Cache plug-in is disabled. Click the link in the notice to go to the WP Super Cache admin page to configure it **A**.

3. From the Easy tab of the WP Super Cache Settings screen, you will see the option to turn caching on. Select Caching On (Recommended), and click Update Status **B**.

continues on next page

WP Super Cache is disabled. Please go to the plugin admin page to enable caching.

A Click the "plugin admin page" link in the WP Super Cache notification to access the configuration options.

WP Super Cache Settings

| Easy | Advanced | CDN | Contents | Preload | Plugins | Debug |

Caching   ● Caching On *(Recommended)*
    ○ Caching Off
    Note: enables PHP caching, cache rebuild, and mobile support

Update Status »

B Choose Caching On (Recommended), and click Update Status to enable caching.

4. For more fine-grained configuration options, click the Advanced tab. You will see many options, with recommendations next to the ones the plug-in author suggests **C**.

| Easy | **Advanced** | CDN | Contents | Preload | Plugins | Debug |

Caching
☑ Cache hits to this website for quick access. *(Recommended)*

○ Use mod_rewrite to serve cache files. *(Recommended)*
◉ Use PHP to serve cache files.
○ Legacy page caching.
Mod_rewrite is fastest, PHP is almost as fast and easier to get working, while legacy caching is slower again, but more flexible and also easy to get working. New users should use PHP caching.

Miscellaneous
☐ Compress pages so they're served more quickly to visitors. *(Recommended)*
Compression is disabled by default because some hosts have problems with compressed files. Switching it on and off clears the cache.
☐ 304 Not Modified browser caching. Indicate when a page has not been modified since last requested. *(Recommended)*
304 support is disabled by default because some hosts have had problems with the headers used in the past.
☐ Don't cache pages for known users. *(Recommended)*
☐ Don't cache pages with GET parameters. (?x=y at the end of a url)
☐ Make known users anonymous so they're served supercached static files.
☑ Cache rebuild. Serve a supercache file to anonymous users while a new file is being generated. *(Recommended)*
☐ Proudly tell the world your server is <u>Stephen Fry proof</u>! (places a message in your blog's footer)

C Under the Advanced tab, select the advanced caching options you want to enable.

More Ways to Speed Up Your Site

Here are some additional ways to speed up the loading time of your site:

- **Show fewer posts at a time on your blog pages.** Click Settings > Reading Settings in your WordPress admin sidebar to adjust the number of posts that appear on your blog pages.

- **Use fewer images in each post.** Large images and graphics take a long time to load, so using fewer images will speed up your site. If you do need to use lots of images in a post, make sure each image is optimized for the Web and saved at an appropriate size.

- **Minimize the number of embedded videos, graphics, and widgets that appear on each page.** Each time your site needs to query an external site or service, the time your own site takes to load increases. Keep these external media queries to a minimum to ensure zippy loading of your site.

Below these options, you will see more configuration settings **D**. These settings are for handling specific situations, such as enabling lockdown during a major traffic spike or disabling caching for certain page types. Unless your site has a particular need for these options, it's best to leave them configured as is.

5. Click Update Status to save any changes you have made. Visitors to your site will now see cached versions of your pages.

☐ Remove UTF8/blog charset support from .htaccess file. Only necessary if you see odd characters or punctuation looks incorrect. Requires rewrite rules update.

☐ Clear all cache files when a post or page is published or updated.

☐ Extra homepage checks. (Very occasionally stops homepage caching) *(Recommended)*

☐ Only refresh current page when comments made.

☐ List the newest cached pages on this page.

☐ Coarse file locking. You probably don't need this but it may help if your server is underpowered. Warning! *May cause your server to lock up in very rare cases!*

☐ Late init. Display cached files after WordPress has loaded. Most useful in legacy mode.

DO NOT CACHE PAGE secret key: 26c6a44949ed97c43379788553794230

D These additional caching options may be enabled if your site has a special need for them.

Using Stats to Evaluate Traffic

You can get valuable information about your site by checking out statistics showing who is visiting your site, where visitors are coming from, and which pages they're viewing.

In this section, you'll learn how to use the WordPress.com Stats feature, which is part of the Jetpack plug-in you installed in Chapter 15, "More Ways to Customize WordPress."

To use WordPress.com Stats:

1. In your WordPress admin sidebar, click the Jetpack link **A**.

2. Find WordPress.com Stats in the Jetpack menu, and click Configure **B**.

3. Choose your configuration options, and click Save Configuration **C**. You can choose to display a small chart in your Admin Bar showing your latest views, count the views of logged-in users (these are disregarded by default), and select the user levels that can view site stats.

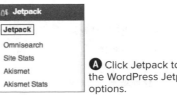

A Click Jetpack to access the WordPress Jetpack plug-in options.

B Find WordPress.com Stats, and click Configure.

C Choose your configuration options, and click Save Configuration.

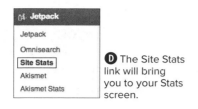

D The Site Stats link will bring you to your Stats screen.

4. To view your stats, click the Site Stats link in the Jetpack menu in your WordPress admin sidebar **D**.

You will see an overview of your latest site traffic, as well as five categories of statistics: Referrers, Top Posts & Pages, Search Engine Terms, Clicks, and Incoming Links **E**.

2. Search Engine Terms

5. Clicks

3. Graph showing site traffic

4. Top Posts & Pages

1. Referrers

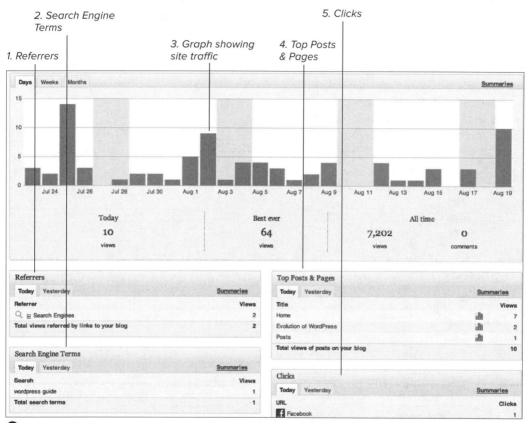

E The WordPress.com Stats screen. Note that the final category, Incoming Links, is not pictured.

Backing Up Your Data and Files

Regular backups are an integral part of the ongoing maintenance for your Web site. The consequences of losing a site's worth of data can range from annoying to potentially disastrous, especially if you're using WordPress to run a Web site for your business.

To perform a full backup of all your data as well as your themes and plug-ins, you'll need to make copies of two very different things: the data in your MySQL database and the files that make up your WordPress installation. We'll show you how to do this with a simple FTP download of the site files using the popular phpMyAdmin tool to back up your database.

You can find a wealth of information on various WordPress backup methods in the WordPress Codex: http://codex.wordpress.org/WordPress_Backups.

To back up your data:

1. Sign in to phpMyAdmin on your hosting account. The URL you'll need to use for this varies from host to host.

2. Click Databases to display a list of databases on your server. The list should include the database you used when you installed WordPress. If you have multiple WordPress sites, you may have stored their data in one or more databases Ⓐ. Click the Export tab to continue.

continues on next page

Ⓐ The phpMyAdmin databases screen lists all of the databases on your hosting account.

3. The next screen contains many fields. Most of these can be left alone, but a few must be filled out. In the Export box, select any WordPress databases you wish to back up. Make sure that the export type is set to SQL and that the Add DROP TABLE / VIEW / PROCEDURE / FUNCTION and Save As File check boxes are both selected. Click Go to continue **B**.

4. Save the .sql file generated by phpMyAdmin to your computer. Your data is backed up. Now you should back up your site files.

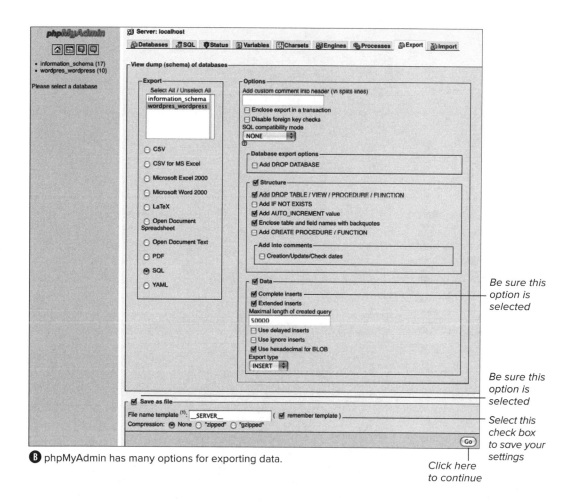

B phpMyAdmin has many options for exporting data.

Be sure this option is selected

Be sure this option is selected

Select this check box to save your settings

Click here to continue

To back up your site files:

1. Open your favorite FTP client, enter the settings provided to you by your hosting company, and sign in. You should see a list of files and directories on your local computer as well as on your Web server **C**. Navigate to the directory where you installed WordPress on your Web host or server.

2. Create a new directory (wordpress in our example) on your computer. This is where you will be downloading all your site files **D**.

C This screen contains a list of files and directories on your local computer and on your Web server.

D Drag all of your WordPress files and directories to a directory on your local computer to begin the backup process.

3. Drag all of the WordPress files from the server to the directory you just created. Wait for them to finish downloading **E**. Most FTP clients will notify you when the job is done by playing a sound or displaying a pop-up window.

4. Locate the directory you created on your local computer's file system **F**. Notice that we've placed the file directory in the same location as our data backup file (localhost.sql). This way we can compress them together, which will make restoring the backup much easier if it is needed.

continues on next page

E The FTP backup files have been downloaded.

F The backup directory you created earlier is now full of your site's files.

5. Select the files you want to compress and right-click (Ctrl-click on a Mac) to open the context menu. Compress (or archive, or ZIP on some systems) the files to create one archival file containing both the directory of files and your data backup file **G**.

The compressed file (Archive.zip in our example) will appear in the directory **H**. Your backup is complete; just make sure you save that .zip file in case you need it later.

Using VaultPress

VaultPress is a service created by Automattic (the company behind WordPress.com) that automatically and regularly backs up your entire WordPress installation for a monthly fee. You can activate the VaultPress service through the Jetpack plug-in **I** (see Chapter 15, "More Ways to Customize WordPress," for instructions on activating Jetpack add-ons).

G Archive (ZIP) your backup.

H The compressed backup file will take up less room and be easier to send to tech support personnel if need be.

I Click Learn More to begin the process of setting up VaultPress for your site.

Once you activate the add-on and set up your VaultPress account, you will be able to view your backup status and link to your VaultPress account from your WordPress dashboard **J**. If your site goes down, you will be able to log directly in to VaultPress to restore to the last saved backup **K**.

Learn more about VaultPress by visiting vaultpress.com.

J The VaultPress screen in your WordPress admin area gives you an overview of your backup status.

K Your backups are stored securely on the VaultPress site and can be restored to your site with the click of a button.

Putting It All Together

1. **Install the All In One SEO Pack plug-in.** How do you configure the plug-in options? Where do you enter information specific to a post or a page?

2. **Copy and paste some text from a Word document into a new post.** How can you do this without including extra markup? Where is the Paste From Word button?

3. **Check your plug-ins.** Have you installed any plug-ins that you are not using? How do you disable them?

4. **Install WP Super Cache.** What does this plug-in do? How do you configure it?

5. **Back up your content.** Why is it important to create regular backups?

Troubleshooting

In this section, we'll help out with some common WordPress problems and point you in the right direction for finding answers online.

Nothing Happens

My changes aren't showing up!

If you're not seeing changes you make to your site, try these tips:

Empty your browser's cache

Have you emptied your cache? Sometimes, to save time and resources, your browser will show you a previously captured, or *cached*, version of a page. You can clear your browser's cache and force the page to reload by following these instructions.

Microsoft Internet Explorer

While pressing the Shift key, click the Refresh button in the toolbar.

For serious clearing: If you are having problems clearing the cache, you can force it by choosing Tools > Delete Browsing History to open the Delete Browsing History dialog box. Select the Temporary Internet Files check box, and click Delete.

Mozilla Firefox

Hold down Ctrl+Shift+R (Command+Shift+R on a Mac).

For serious clearing: From the browser's menu, choose Tools and select Clear Recent History. In the drop-down menu for "Time range to clear," select Everything, and click Clear Now .

Google Chrome

From the browser's menu, click Chrome > Clear Browsing Data.

Ⓐ Select Everything from the drop-down menu to clear your entire cache in Firefox.

Safari	File	Edit	View	Histor

About Safari
Safari Extensions...

Report Bugs to Apple...

Preferences...   ⌘,
Block Pop–Up Windows ⇧⌘K

Private Browsing...
Reset Safari...
Empty Cache...   ⌥⌘E

Services   ▶

Hide Safari   ⌘H
Hide Others   ⌥⌘H
Show All

Quit Safari   ⌘Q

B Choose Reset Safari to clear your cache in Safari.

Safari

From the browser's menu, choose Safari > Reset Safari **B**, and click Reset to confirm.

or

Choose Safari > Empty Cache.

Check your caching plug-ins

Are you using a caching plug-in to speed up your site? Plug-ins like WP-Super Cache can create a delay between when you make an update and when it shows on the front end of your site. Check your plug-in's instructions for specific details on how to clear its cache.

Make sure you're editing the right template

Double-check to be sure the template file you're editing is the correct one. Some template files have very similar code, and it can be difficult to know which one applies to which page on your site. Check out the template hierarchy page on the WordPress Codex to be sure you're editing the correct template file: http://codex.wordpress.org/Template_Hierarchy

TIP The template trace extension for the debug bar plug-in adds an option to the admin bar that can help identify the current file being displayed. http://wordpress.org/support/plugin/debug-bar-template-trace

All browsers

If the previous troubleshooting tips don't solve the problem, check your source code. Something as simple as a tag that was never closed can keep a page from loading correctly.

If none of these methods work for you, check out the detailed instructions on the WordPress Codex for more in-depth troubleshooting: http://codex.wordpress.org/I_Make_Changes_and_Nothing_Happens.

Overwriting Changes

Changes I made to the WordPress default theme were lost during the last automatic upgrade!

A core update copies all the new files from the distribution over the old ones—including files in the WordPress default theme. That means if you changed existing files in the WordPress default theme, those changes got overwritten when you upgraded. There isn't a fix for this, but we can offer advice to make sure it doesn't happen again!

To prevent loss of theme changes during an upgrade:

1. Create a child theme instead of modifying the default theme. Child themes allow you to make changes to specific template files and functions while using the parent theme as a default. Learn more about creating child themes at http://codex.wordpress.org/Child_Themes.

2. Activate your child theme, and add changes to it rather than to the default theme.

TIP **Always back up your files and database before an upgrade.**

Updates

An update to WordPress was just released, so why doesn't my blog recognize that the update is available?

Looking for that release notification at the top of your admin screen? Not every site will see that message at the same time. Your WordPress site is programmed to check for updates every 12 hours, so if an update was released right after the last check, it may be a while before you are notified.

You can force the issue if you really need that update right away.

To update your site before you receive an update notification:

1. In your Web-hosting control panel (cPanel), access the MySQL database for your WordPress installation.

2. In the MySQL database, delete the **update_core** option name record in your *wp_options* table. That will cause your WordPress installation to check immediately for an update rather than waiting the remainder of the time from the last check.

Admin Access

I can't access the administrative menus!

If you were able to access the admin area in the past but can't now, a bad plug-in may be to blame. To identify the culprit, you'll need to deactivate all your plug-ins, and then add them back one by one.

A Rename the plugins folder to deactivate all your plug-ins.

To deactivate all plug-ins:

1. Create an empty plug-ins folder on your computer.

2. In your FTP client, navigate to the wp-content directory.

3. Rename the plugins folder to plugins. hold **A**.

4. Upload the empty plugins folder you created in step 1 to the wp-content directory.

5. Log in to your WordPress admin area and click Plugins in the sidebar menu. Because your plugins folder is empty, WordPress automatically deactivates all your plug-ins **B**.

B In the Plugins screen of your WordPress admin area, you will see that all of your plug-ins have been deactivated.

6. In your FTP client, delete the empty plugins folder you uploaded in step 4.

7. Rename the plugins.hold folder back to plugins.

8. In your administrative area, refresh the Plugins section. You will see all your old plug-ins in the list ready for you to activate them **C**.

9. Activate plug-ins one by one to find the culprit that caused the initial access problem.

Plugins Add New

All (10) I Inactive (10) I Update Available (4)

Search Installed Plugins

Bulk Actions ⬍ Apply

10 items

	Plugin	Description
☐	**Akismet** Activate I Edit I Delete	Used by millions, Akismet is quite possibly the best way in the world to **protect your blog from comment and trackback spam**. It keeps your site protected from spam even while you sleep. To get started: 1) Click the "Activate" link to the left of this description, 2) Sign up for an Akismet API key, and 3) Go to your Akismet configuration page, and save your API key. Version 2.5.3 I By Automattic I Visit plugin site
☐	**All in One SEO Pack** Activate I Edit I Delete	Out-of-the-box SEO for your Wordpress blog. Options configuration panel I Upgrade to Pro Version I Donate I Support I Amazon Wishlist Version 1.6.13.3 I By Michael Torbert I Visit plugin site
☐	**Disqus Comment System** Activate I Edit I Delete	The Disqus comment system replaces your WordPress comment system with your comments hosted and powered by Disqus. Head over to the Comments admin page to set up your DISQUS Comment System. Version 2.66 I By Disqus I Visit plugin site
☐	**Easy Featured Image** Activate I Edit I Delete	This plugin enables editing the featured images on the edit.php in the admin menu. You will need to put this in your functions.php to enable featured images:<?php add_theme_support('post-thumbnails'); Version 1.1 I By Robert Braam I Visit plugin site
☐	**Hello Dolly** Activate I Edit I Delete	This is not just a plugin, it symbolizes the hope and enthusiasm of an entire generation summed up in two words sung most famously by Louis Armstrong: Hello, Dolly. When activated you will randomly see a lyric from Hello, Dolly in the upper right of your admin screen on every page. Version 1.6 I By Matt Mullenweg I Visit plugin site
☐	**Jetpack by WordPress.com** Activate I Edit I Delete	Bring the power of the WordPress.com cloud to your self-hosted WordPress. Jetpack enables you to connect your blog to a WordPress.com account to use the powerful features normally only available to WordPress.com users. Version 1.1.2 I By Automattic I Visit plugin site
☐	**Related Posts Thumbnails** Activate I Edit I Delete	Showing related posts thumbnails under the post. Version 1.3 I By Maria Shaldybina I Visit plugin site
☐	**Slimbox** Activate I Edit I Delete	Enables slimbox 2 on all image links including BMP, GIF, JPG, JPEG, and PNG links. Version 1.0.6 I By Kevin Sylvestre I Visit plugin site
☐	**TF Maintenance Mode** Activate I Edit I Delete	Adds a maintenance-page to your site that lets visitors know your site is down for maintenancetime. Version 1.0.0 I By Themefuse I Visit plugin site
☐	**WooTumblog** Activate I Edit I Delete	Create a tumblr style blog using this plugin. Version 2.0.4 I By Jeffikus of WooThemes I Visit plugin site

C After deleting the empty plugins folder and renaming the original folder back to plugins, you will be able to reactivate your plug-ins one by one.

Commenting Problems

Why do I get a blank page when I submit a comment?

If a blank page appears when a comment is submitted and the comment does not show up on your site, your theme may be missing a critical part of the comment form. Check the comments.php file in your theme and ensure that the following code appears within the form:

```
<input type="hidden"
→ name="comment_post_ID"
→ value="<?php echo $id; ?>" />
```

If the code is not there, enter it just below the code for the Submit button.

Online Help Resources

WordPress Codex Troubleshooting FAQ: http://codex.wordpress.org/FAQ_Troubleshooting

WordPress forums: http://wordpress.org/support

Where Do I Go for Help?

If you get stuck with a WordPress problem you can't easily resolve, there are lots of ways to find the answers you need.

Get online and start researching. The WordPress site provides user forums and excellent documentation that can offer the assistance you need.

If you have a specific error or problem, try inputting the error message directly into a search engine. Chances are someone else has encountered the error and has posted a solution online.

Get to know other WordPress users in your local area; they can be a great resource. Many regional groups maintain their own forums or mailing lists where you can get help.

B

Online Resources

There are lots of online resources that can provide valuable information about WordPress. We have compiled a list of some of our favorites, as well as some of the tools we use for blogging, designing, and coding WordPress sites.

For a comprehensive list of resources, you can visit this book's companion site at http://wpvisualquickstart.com.

WordPress Information

WordPress.org (Official Site):
http://wordpress.org

WordPress.com:
http://en.wordpress.com

WordPress Codex:
http://codex.wordpress.org

WordPress Forums:
http://wordpress.org/support

WordPress Requirements:
http://wordpress.org/about/requirements

WordPress Web Hosting:
http://wordpress.org/hosting

Using Themes:
http://codex.wordpress.org/Using_Themes

Free Themes Directory:
http://wordpress.org/extend/themes

Templates:
http://codex.wordpress.org/Templates

Template Hierarchy:
http://codex.wordpress.org/Template_Hierarchy

Template Tags:
http://codex.wordpress.org/Template_Tags

Custom Post Types:
http://codex.wordpress.org/Post_Types

Custom Taxonomies:
http://codex.wordpress.org/Taxonomies

Extend (Plug-in Directory):
http://wordpress.org/extend

Other Resources

These links and applications and plug-ins may not have been developed by WordPress, but they can greatly enhance your blogging experience.

Backups

VaultPress:
http://vaultpress.com/

Blog editors

MarsEdit:
http://red-sweater.com/marsedit/

Windows Essentials Writer:
http://windows.microsoft.com/en-us/
windows-live/essentials-other

Ecto:
http://illuminex.com/ecto/

Browsers

Firefox:
http://getfirefox.com

Chrome:
http://chrome.com

Opera:
www.opera.com

Color schemes

Colour Lovers:
www.colourlovers.com

Kuler:
http://kuler.adobe.com

Favicon generator

Favikon:
http://favikon.com

MySQL

MySQL & MySQL Administrator:
http://mysql.com

PHP

PHP:
http://php.net

WordCamp conference schedule

http://central.wordcamp.org/

WordPress plug-ins

All In One SEO Pack:
http://wordpress.org/extend/plugins/
all-in-one-seo-pack

Disqus:
http://wordpress.org/extend/plugins/
disqus-comment-system/

IntenseDebate:
http://wordpress.org/extend/plugins/
intensedebate/

WP Super Cache:
http://wordpress.org/extend/plugins/
wp-super-cache

WP Touch Pro:
http://www.bravenewcode.com/store/
plugins/wptouch-pro/

WordPress TV how-to videos

http://wordpress.tv/category/how-to/

Pattern generators

BGPatterns:
http://bgpatterns.com/

Stripe Generator:
http://www.stripegenerator.com/

Podcatchers

iTunes:
www.apple.com/itunes

Juice:
http://juicereceiver.sourceforge.net/

Spelling and grammar

After the Deadline:
http://afterthedeadline.com/

Typography

Type-a-file:
http://www.type-a-file.com/

Typetester:
www.typetester.org

Typograph:
http://lamb.cc/typograph/

Validators

W3C Validator
http://validator.w3.org

Web fonts

FontsLive:
http://www.fontslive.com/catalog/

Google Web Fonts:
http://www.google.com/webfonts

TypeKit:
http://typekit.com/

Index

plug-ins, 93
tags, 113–114
users on network, 221–222
media, 133–152. *See also* images; Media Library;
    video files
    adding to post, 97
    editing images, 139–141
    managing image galleries, 142–145
    saving edited images, 141
    uploading, 134–138
    using audio and video files, 146–151
Media Library
    choosing header image from, 77
    experimenting with, 152
    selecting background image from, 79
    uploading files from, 134–138
Menu Settings area, 127
menus, 125–132. *See also* cPanel
    adding to sites, 129
    assigning to theme location, 129, 132
    creating, 128, 132
    customizing, 65, 126–127
    deleting items on, 127
    editing, 130–131
    hovering over items on, 26, 28
    options for, 132
    reordering items on, 132
    Settings, 36
    styling items on, 171–172
    supporting custom, 179
    unable to access admin, 260–261
metadata, 168
moderating comments, 155–157, 159–161
More tag, 105
multiple blogs
    adding plug-ins for, 222
    administering blog network, 220–221
    changing default theme for, 222–223, 224
    managing users on network, 221–222
    support for, 213
My Sites link, 217
MySQL database, 7–8

N

naming databases, 7, 8
navigation. *See also* menus
    sitemaps, 241
    Twenty Thirteen default, 67

networked blogs
    adding, 219
    administering, 220–221
    changing default theme for, 222–223
    knowledge required to run, 213
    plug-ins for, 222
notification preference, 156

O

online resources
    blogging and site, 265–266
    book's companion site, 263
    color, 169, 265
    theme development, 184
    troubleshooting, 262
    WordPress, 264
opening
    Posts screen, 28
    Theme Customizer, 73
Other WordPress News module, 23

P

pages. *See also* themes
    adding, 101–103
    audio files added to, 147
    creating, 124
    defined, 101
    displaying custom post types, 206–207, 212
    editing, 104–105
    embedding video in, 150–151, 152, 245
    entering contact information for, 54
    images on, 136–138
    linking to, 106
    reverting to previous version, 107–108
    Sample, 27, 28
    setting up static front, 50
    subpages for, 103
    themes for, 68
    video files added to, 148–149
parent categories, 110, 111
parent pages, 103
passwords. *See also* username
    automatically generated, 7–8, 15
    changing, 16–17
    Fantastico, 4
    phpMyAdmin, 9
    recommendations for, 54
    sending new user's, 57